The Gospel in Job

Yannick Ford

Scripture Truth Publications

Some of this material appeared in articles published in "Scripture Truth" magazine 2004-2006.

FIRST EDITION

FIRST PRINTING March 2007

ISBN: 978-0-901860-76-7 (paperback)

ISBN: 978-0-901860-77-4 (hardback)

© Copyright 2007 Yannick Ford/Scripture Truth

A publication of Scripture Truth

Scripture quotations marked (NKJV) are taken from the New King James Version®. Copyright © 1982 by Thomas Nelson, Inc. Used by permission. All rights reserved.

Scripture quotations marked "J. N. Darby translation" are taken from "The Holy Scriptures, a New Translation from the Original Languages" by J. N. Darby (G Morrish, 1890).

Cover photograph ©iStockphoto.com/plefevre (Paul LeFevre)

Published by Scripture Truth Publications
Coopies Way, Coopies Lane,
Morpeth, Northumberland, NE61 6JN

Scripture Truth is an imprint of Central Bible Hammond Trust, a charitable trust

Typesetting by John Rice
Printed by Lightning Source

Contents

THE GOSPEL IN JOB

1. Introduction

The book of Job has attracted me for a long time, for a number of reasons. It is a very old book, and is thought to relate incidents that took place in patriarchal times, such as in the times of Abraham [1]. The majority of the book is taken up with the lengthy sayings of Job and his friends, which must be profitable for us, as we read in 1 Timothy 3:16[a], and yet I have not found many commentaries dealing in detail with these. Most importantly, the great truths of the gospel, the good news of God's love towards us and His provision for our sin, are clearly brought out in this book. So too are the activities of Satan, and his ultimate defeat by God.

It is these latter reasons that encouraged me to write a commentary, that is to set out the gospel of the grace of God as seen in the book of Job. There is also a parallel strand to this, which we will see. The New Testament teaches us that our *sins* can be forgiven, and so we can be made right with God — that is the beginning of the gospel of the grace of God. But the New Testament further teaches us that the root cause of our sins, *our sinful nature*, has also been dealt with. The Biblical expression for our sinful nature is "sin in the flesh", and we are told that it has been condemned at the cross of Jesus (Romans 8:3). Practically speaking, this is often not such an easy concept to grasp. There are many issues surrounding this truth, but at this point we can just consider the fact that we *cannot* stand before God in *our own merits or strength*. Job needed to learn this, and so we will see this point brought out in this book. I have therefore regularly mentioned these two major strands (the gospel that brings us forgiveness of sins, and the need to understand that our sinful nature has also been dealt with), since they are illustrated in many different ways. I trust that the reader will not be put off by seeming repetition. The way that God teaches us through His Word, the Bible, is very often "Precept upon precept, precept upon precept, Line upon line, line upon line, Here a little, there a little" (see Isaiah 28:13, NKJV). The truths of God are never too complicated for our intellect, but they are often difficult for our *pride*! And so, we are taught "here a little, there a little" as we read through the Bible, so that we will learn to assimilate these truths, and they will become part of us.

Job's friends also play a major part. Their arguments with Job take up the majority of the book! They did not understand that Job was a good man, a servant of God, who nevertheless needed to learn not to trust in his own righteousness. Their main thrust, as we will see, was that Job must have committed some serious sin for God to have brought Job's sufferings on him. As such they were not helpful to Job[b]. Indeed, the expression 'Job's comforters' has become proverbial for those who try to sympathise with you, whilst at the same time suggesting that you have brought your problems on yourself. It is important to realise that while Job's friends said many *true* things, most were not *applied* in the right way.

The book of Job was originally written in Hebrew, like the majority of the Old Testament. Substantial parts of this book are in poetical form. Hebrew poetry does not rhyme, as some English poetry does (and anyway it would be exceedingly difficult to translate Hebrew into English while maintaining rhyme!) Instead, as explained by Ray E. Baughman [2], there is a rhyming of ideas, known technically as parallelism. Baughman distinguishes three types of parallelism: (i) the second line repeats the meaning of the first line; (ii) the second line adds meaning or explains the first line; (iii) the second is opposite in meaning from the first line. Job 40:18 is an example of the first type: "His bones are as strong pieces of brass; his bones are like bars of iron." This type of poetic structure can of course be translated into any language without loss.

I trust that this commentary will be of help to those reading the book of Job in the Bible, and that it will stimulate the reading and further study of this book. I would like to acknowledge those authors whose writings have helped and influenced me, and shaped my thoughts for this book, viz. C.H. Mackintosh's commentary on Job [8], the writings of F.C. Jennings (e.g. reference [3]), and also Roy Hession [9].

Notes

- In general, quotes from the Bible are taken from the New King James Version, and this is noted as 'NKJV'. Occasionally I have quoted from a Bible translation produced in the 19th century by Mr J.N.Darby, which more exactly translates the original manuscripts.
- Within NKJV quotations, words or phrases added by the translators in order to give the full meaning of the original text are shown in *italics*.

- In certain quotes I have emphasised selected words or phrases in **bold type**.
- Endnotes are labelled as superscripted letters, e.g. [a].
- References are indicated by numbers in square brackets, e.g. [1].Bibliographic details are given at the end of the commentary.

2. The Unseen Conflict

Job chapters 1 & 2:1-10

Chapter 1 begins by introducing Job, his family, his property and where he lived. Verse 1 tells us that Job was "perfect and upright, and one that feared God and abstained from evil" (J. N. Darby translation). What does it mean to say the Job was 'perfect'? Noah was also described as perfect[a], and Abraham was called to be perfect[b]. 'Perfect' does not mean sinless or absolute perfection, but rather suggests the idea of completeness and maturity. Luke 6:40, Ephesians 4:13, Colossians 4:12, 1 Thessalonians 3:10 and 2 Timothy 3:17 are New Testament examples of the use of the word 'perfect' in the sense of complete, mature or full-grown, and in this sense it is also applied to the Lord Jesus Himself in Hebrews 2:10: "For it was fitting for Him, for whom *are* all things and by whom *are* all things, in bringing many sons to glory, to make the captain of their salvation perfect through sufferings". We can therefore paraphrase verse 1 by saying that Job was an upright man, not lacking or at fault in any obvious way, and in keeping with this he shunned evil.

God had blessed Job with material goods, which was a sign of favour in Old Testament times. He was blessed with children, servants and substance. In our dispensation, those of us who know the Lord Jesus Christ as our Saviour are blessed in spiritual rather than in material ways. Ephesians 1:3 tells us that God our Father has "blessed us with every spiritual blessing in the heavenly *places* in Christ". The challenge for us therefore is whether we know and enjoy these blessings in a real way. Colossians 3:1-2 tells us that "if ye then be risen with Christ, seek those things which are above, where Christ sitteth on the right hand of God. Set your affection on things above, not on things on the earth."

Verses 4 and 5 show Job's concern for the spiritual well-being of his family. Job's sons feasted "every one on his day", which presumably means his birthday. Job was concerned for them that they may have been tempted to curse God during their feasting, and so offered burnt offerings for them all. In the light of the New Testament we know that *in themselves*, sacrifices cannot take away sins, but pointed forward to the death of Christ as atonement for our sins[c].

We are transported to a different scene altogether in verse 6, where we see angels gathered together to give an account of their service to the Lord. Satan also comes with them, so the Lord asks him "From where do you come?" Since God never asks questions for His own benefit, in that He does not need to ask to find out the answer, the question must have been intended as a rebuke for Satan. It is worthwhile digressing a little here to point out some common misconceptions regarding Satan and his activities. The western world largely does not believe in the existence of Satan, or else he is regarded as some evil, mythological type of character, often portrayed with goat's feet and tail, and thought to rule over his demons in the kingdom of hell. It is beyond the scope of this study to go into great detail as to the truth about Satan, but I would recommend F. C. Jennings' excellent treatment of this subject [3]. A quotation from Sir Robert Anderson's book "The Silence of God" [4] is very apt at this point:

> The devil of Christendom is a myth. . . . The Satan of Christian mythology is a monster of wickedness, the instigator to every crime of exceptional brutality or loathsome lust. The Satan of Scripture is the awful being who dared to offer his patronage to our Divine Lord. . . . The Satan of Scripture is a being who claimed to meet our Lord on more than equal terms. . . . Men dream of a devil, horned and hoofed — a hideous and obscene monster — who haunts the squalid slums and gilded vice-dens of our cities, and tempts the depraved to acts of atrocity and shame. But, according to Holy Writ, he "fashions himself into an angel of light" and "his ministers fashion themselves as ministers of righteousness" [2 Corinthians 11: 14]. . . . it is the *religion* of the world that he controls, and not its vices and its crimes. "The god of this world" is his awful title — a title Divinely conceded to the Evil One, not because the Supreme has delegated His sovereignty, but because the world accords him its homage. It is in the sphere of religion, then, that the influence of the Tempter is to be sought — not in the records of our criminal courts, not in the pages of obscene novels, but in the teachings of false theologies.

Satan is not reigning in hell. The Bible tells us that Satan will be cast into hell in the future[d], and that, far from being Satan's kingdom, hell has been prepared for him as his punishment[e]. It is worth stressing this fact: that hell was prepared specifically for the *devil and his angels*. It is not God's desire that any *persons* should end up there[f]. The fact that some will is a tragedy of their own making, since full provision has been made so that *no-one needs to go there*, as we shall see as we go through the book of Job. The death of Christ is sufficient for all who desire the forgiveness of their sins[g].

At present, however, Satan is 'at large', so to speak, and these chapters of Job show us his activities. The name 'Satan' means 'adversary' [1], and this gives a clue as to his character. Satan, as our adversary, accuses us before God[h], as we see graphically portrayed in the passage below (Zechariah 3:1-5, NKJV):

> Then he showed me Joshua the high priest standing before the Angel of the LORD, and Satan standing at his right hand to oppose him. And the LORD said to Satan, "The LORD rebuke you, Satan! The LORD who has chosen Jerusalem rebuke you! *Is* this not a brand plucked from the fire?" Now Joshua was clothed with filthy garments, and was standing before the Angel. Then He answered and spoke to those who stood before Him, saying, "Take away the filthy garments from him." And to him He said, "See, I have removed your iniquity from you, and I will clothe you with rich robes." And I said, "Let them put a clean turban on his head." So they put a clean turban on his head, and they put the clothes on him. And the Angel of the LORD stood by.

Satan's accusations of us are, alas, not groundless, as shown figuratively in the above passage by Joshua's filthy clothes. We are all too aware of our failings and sins that could be brought to God's attention. Satan's object in presenting them to God is not merely to cause our misery, but he aims to strike at the character of God Himself. It is as if he is saying to God "How can You, a holy God, show mercy to these sinners, whose sins are so evident? Surely this denies Your character of holiness?" And so he would seek to place God in a dilemma, where He cannot exercise mercy in keeping with His character of love, while at the same time maintain absolute righteousness in keeping with His character of holiness. But in the New Testament we have the wonderful truth that God's judgement for sin was borne by the Lord Jesus Christ Himself, so that we can now be justified in God's sight, without affecting His holiness[i]. This is foreshadowed in the passage quoted above, where God can rebuke Satan and tell Joshua that He has caused his iniquity to pass away from him.

> *No act of power could e'er atone,*
> *No wonder-working word*
> *Could, from the brightness of the throne,*
> *Make love's sweet voice be heard.*
>
> *If sinners ever were to know*
> *The depths of love divine,*
> *All Calvary's weakness and its woe,*
> *Blest Saviour, must be Thine.*
>
> *God's righteousness is there proclaimed,*
> *His mercy's depths are known,*
> *While to the full Thou hast maintained*
> *The glory of His throne.*
>
> *God now is glorified in Thee,*
> *In Thee, His only Son;*
> *His hand, His house, His heart are free,*
> *Because Thy work is done.*

C. A. Coates (1862 - 1945)

Returning to our study of Job, we see in verse 8 that God challenges Satan with Job's exemplary behaviour. Satan however insinuates that Job's good conduct is simply a result of his material blessing. It is interesting that Satan refers to God 'hedging Job about'. This gives us an insight into God's protection, and shows us that Satan is unable to do anything towards us beyond that specifically permitted by God — God remains in ultimate control. We see this again in verse 12: in response to Satan's retort, God allows Satan to afflict Job's possessions, but he is not allowed to touch Job himself. Verses 13 - 19 underline Satan's malevolent character as we see how rapidly he carries out his mission. Note the expression in verse 16, where the messenger refers to the "fire of God [that] fell from heaven", whereas we know from the context that it was initiated by Satan.

Satan had said that Job would curse God to His face, but Job's reaction to this series of disasters is exemplary. Verse 21 is very true — we enter this world with nothing, and can take nothing with us when we leave it. The apostle Paul says the same in 1 Timothy 6:7 "For we brought nothing into *this* world, *and it is* certain we can carry nothing out." The Lord Jesus Himself alludes to this in Luke 12:15 "And He said to them, "Take heed and beware of covetousness, for one's life does not consist in the abundance of the things he possesses."" Still, how many of us would be able to react as Job did?

Satan presents himself to God again in chapter 2, and once again God challenges him with Job's conduct. Satan, who still desires to see Job curse God, now suggests that Job will not remain in his integrity if his health is affected. And so once more, we see Satan rapidly fulfilling his desire, and Job is afflicted with a painful illness. Verse 9 shows us Job's own wife tempting Job to curse God, but still Job does not sin with his lips.

Satan was defeated — not once did Job curse God, even though he lost all his family, possessions, and his health. In fact we do not hear directly any more of Satan in the book of Job. However, we must ask ourselves if there was not a deeper reason for Job's trial than the defeat of Satan in his attempt to cause Job to curse God. In a sense, God initiated the situation by bringing Job to Satan's attention. We need to be careful in our argument here, as James 1:13 tells us that "Let no one say when he is tempted, "I am tempted by God"; for God cannot be tempted by evil, nor does He Himself tempt anyone." It was Satan that brought about Job's suffering, and sought to lead Job to curse God. Satan displayed his character of evil in his response to God's challenge and in his dealings with Job. Nevertheless, God *allowed* Satan to act, within defined limits, for a deeper purpose, and for Job's ultimate blessing, as we shall see as we continue our study.

3. Job's first complaint

JOB CHAPTERS 2:11-13 & 3

The next section in the story of Job begins with the arrival of his three friends: Eliphaz the Temanite, Bildad the Shuhite and Zophar the Naamathite. These three must have been deeply affected by what they saw, for they did not speak for seven days. After this, Job cursed the day of his birth. His complaint is bitter and full of anguished questions. We can divide it into three sections: verses 1 - 10, where Job curses the day he was born because he did not die then; verses 11 - 24, where Job speaks of the advantages of death; and verses 25 - 26, in which Job mentions his earlier fears. Let us look at these sections in turn.

Today we have the New Testament that informs us clearly as to what lies beyond death. Before this revelation men and women had only very shadowy ideas about this subject. Prosperity in this life was looked on as evidence of God's blessing, but the grave and beyond was unclear territory[a]. Job had some knowledge of a future resurrection, as we will see in Job chapter 19, and so did Martha of Bethany, when she spoke with the Lord Jesus about the death of her brother Lazarus[b]. Nevertheless, their knowl-

16

edge was very limited, which may explain why Job would rather not have been born than go through the trouble he was now experiencing. Jeremiah the prophet also expressed himself in a similar fashion[c].

When the Lord Jesus was here on this earth, He drew back the curtain to reveal more exactly our future state. We should seriously consider the account of Lazarus and the rich man in the New Testament (Luke 16:19-31). Here we have strikingly presented *two possibilities* — two very different destinations after the death of the body. The time to choose and fix our future destination is *now*[d], and I hope that through this study of Job we will see how each one can be certain of attaining the heavenly destination, and not the place of torment.

If we are assured of heaven, we can consider the words of the Apostle Paul, who said "For our light affliction, which is but for a moment, is working for us a far more exceeding *and* eternal weight of glory, while we do not look at the things which are seen, but at the things which are not seen. For the things which are seen *are* temporary, but the things which are not seen *are* eternal." (2 Corinthians 4:17-18, NKJV) and "For I consider that the sufferings of this present time are not worthy *to be compared* with the glory which shall be revealed in us." (Romans 8:18, NKJV). These are very different statements to Job's cursing the day of birth. Of course, it is easy to make this comment: few of us have had to suffer as Job did. Nevertheless, we know that there *will* be a time when all will be well, and we know that there *is* a purpose to our suffering[e]. Considering the glory that is ahead of us, how could we seriously curse the day of our birth?

Job however did not have the benefit of New Testament revelation. In verses 11-24 of chapter 3, he expresses how

17

death would have been preferable to what he is now experiencing. In a sense, he describes what we might call the popular view of death — rest from the trouble and difficulties of this life. For example, in verses 17-19 he says "There the wicked cease *from* troubling, And there the weary are at rest. *There* the prisoners rest together; They do not hear the voice of the oppressor. The small and great are there, And the servant *is* free from his master." However, as I have already mentioned regarding Lazarus and the rich man in Luke 19, death is not simply a release from suffering and rest from trouble. In the case of the rich man, it was anything but that. ""*There is* no peace," says the LORD, "for the wicked."" (Isaiah 48:22, NKJV; see also 57:21). These thoughts put a rather different light on the idea of seeking death as a release from earthly circumstances.

In the last two verses of this chapter, Job confesses that prior to all his troubles, he had not been in complete security and confidence: "For the thing I greatly feared has come upon me, And what I dreaded has happened to me. I am not at ease, nor am I quiet; I have no rest, for trouble comes." (verses 25-26, NKJV). Similarly today, in spite of all the modern systems that we use to try and secure our future, such as insurance, pension schemes and so on, we still cannot predict every outcome. But if we learn anything from the book of Job, it is that we can *count on God*, and that all is in His control. Adverse circumstances may come along, but they do not hinder His purpose.

4. Eliphaz's first speech and Job's reply

JOB CHAPTERS 4 - 7

We now come to the main part of the book of Job, in which Job's three friends speak about Job and his sufferings, and Job replies to their arguments. Eliphaz begins by accusing Job of self-righteousness (chapter 4 verses 1 - 6). The thrust of his argument seems to be that Job had helped others when they were in trouble, but that now he didn't like trouble himself. But was Eliphaz helping Job by saying this?

Eliphaz speaks mainly from his own experience. In verse 8 he says "Even as *I* have seen ..."; in verse 12 it is "Now a word was secretly brought to *me* ...". Our experience can sometimes be of help, but in general it is not a firm foundation on which to build arguments concerning important issues. Some of what Eliphaz has to say is true, and is even quoted elsewhere in the Bible. However, the *application* of it to Job was not right. We see this in verses 7 - 11, where Eliphaz states that it is the wicked who are punished, with the implication being that Job must have committed some crime, otherwise he would not be suffering his misfortunes. While it is true that we will reap what we sow, as Eliphaz states in verse 8[a], we know from God's own words about Job's character in Job chapters 1 and 2 that Job had not committed some great wickedness. Indeed, as we will discuss later on, sometimes the wicked appear to succeed in their schemes — I say 'appear', as ultimately no-one can escape God's judgement of his life. However, just because someone is suffering in this life, it is by no means necessarily a consequence of their wrongdoing.

Eliphaz further states in chapter 5 verse 6 that "For affliction does not come from the dust, Nor does trouble spring from the ground", again seeming to imply that evil doesn't just happen — there must be a cause. Job chapters 1 & 2 however reveal to us the origin of Job's sufferings: they were brought about by Satan as a result of his challenge to God.

Eliphaz continues his speech by exhorting Job to look to God (chapter 5 verses 8 - end). His comments in verses 12 - 13 ("He frustrates the devices of the crafty, So that their hands cannot carry out their plans. He catches the wise in their own craftiness, And the counsel of the cunning comes quickly upon them" are quoted in the New Testament[b]. Such words are a comfort to us, as we realise that God will not allow the wicked to succeed in the end, and that their evil plans against us will in fact be their undoing. We have a similar thought in Proverbs 11:18: "The wicked *man* does deceptive work", i.e. a work that deceives him.

Verse 17 ("Behold, happy *is* the man whom God corrects; Therefore do not despise the chastening of the Almighty") is another of Eliphaz's comments that is alluded to in the New Testament[c]. In fact, this comment is a fitting summary of the whole book of Job, in that God was correcting Job for Job's profit, so that Job would realise his true position before God, and not rely on his self-righteousness. However, God was *not* correcting Job for some particular crime, as Eliphaz appeared to suggest.

Finally, Eliphaz ends in verse 27 with "Behold, this we have searched out; It *is* true. Hear it, and know for yourself." This sounds very much like forcing our opinions down someone else's throat! We could paraphrase it as "This is what our research on your case shows, Job; it's quite clear, so listen to us and you will be all right." Even if we think we are right, we always need to be careful and tactful when speaking with others. In the matter of explaining the Christian gospel, the apostle Peter gives us valuable advice: "always *be* ready to *give* a defense to everyone who asks you a reason for the hope that is in you, **with meekness and fear**" (1 Peter 3:15, NKJV; emphasis mine).

What can we conclude from Eliphaz's first speech? Many true things were said (even some comments that have been quoted in the New Testament) but they were not said in a sensitive way, and they were not applied in the right way. Eliphaz gives us a very practical example of what to avoid when seeking to help others in trouble!

Job replies to Eliphaz in chapter 6. Verses 1-7 imply that Eliphaz had not properly considered the *extent* of Job's sufferings. "Can you not see what I am going through?", he seems to ask. "A wild ass or an ox would not normally complain when they are being fed (see verse 5) — it is because I am suffering so much that I am complaining so bitterly." Job then returns to his earlier theme of desiring death (verses 8-13). He feels that he simply does not have the strength to go through.

"To him who is afflicted, kindness *should be shown* by his friend, Even though he forsakes the fear of the Almighty. My brothers have dealt deceitfully like a brook, Like the streams of the brooks that pass away," (verses 14-15, NKJV). Job rebukes his friends for their failure to support him in his trouble. Friends should be expected to show pity to one who is suffering, but like a stream that dries up before we can quench our thirst from it, Eliphaz had not helped Job by his speech. Job complains that he had not asked them to come and try to help him (verses 22-23), and now they were reproving him for some supposed error that he must have committed (verses 24-25). "Tell me then what I have done to deserve this suffering?" he asks (verse 24). Eliphaz's words were true enough, but they did not apply to Job (verse 25), and Job, in his bitterness of spirit, accuses Eliphaz of undermining him (verse 27). A comparison of verses 28 and 21 may suggest that Job had been greatly disfigured by his illness, so that Eliphaz and his friends did not even like to look directly at him. If this was so, how much more hurtful the accusing speech delivered earlier by Eliphaz would have been!

Chapter 7 verses 1-10 bring us further graphic details of Job's sufferings. In verses 11-16 Job turns from Eliphaz and his friends and instead addresses God, in the bitterness of his spirit. "Why can You not just leave me alone?" is his question. However, the dreams and visions that terrified him (verse 14) may well have been due to the devil, rather than God directly. We have already seen in Job chapters 1 and 2 that it was the devil who was directly responsible for all that came to pass, and we saw the hateful speed in which he accomplished it.

It is instructive to compare verses 17-18 with Psalm 8. Job says "What *is* man, that You should exalt him, *That* You should set Your heart on him, That You should visit him every morning, *And* test him every moment?" In other words, "Why, O God, do You bother Yourself about men and women anyway — why can't You just leave me be?" How different this is to the expression of wonder in Psalm 8:3-5 "When I consider Your heavens, the work of Your fingers, The moon and the stars, which You have ordained, What is man that You are mindful of him, And the son of man that You visit him? For You have made him a little lower than the angels, And You have crowned him with glory and honor." Here David, the author of the Psalm, considers God's greatness and His wonderful condescension in caring for men and women. This passage in the Psalms is quoted in the New Testament, where it is applied to the Lord Jesus[d]. Here indeed we see the full expression of God's wonderful condescension, in that the Lord Jesus bothered Himself about us to such an extent that He was willing to come to this earth, in the limitations of a human body, and even to die for us so that *we* might be brought to glory rather than to judgement.

Job however, perhaps understandably, could not see this. He did not want God to look over him. In anguish and irritation, he asks God why He cannot just forgive him (verse 21). This is in fact exactly what God does offer each and every one of us, but it was not such an "easy" thing for God to do. God is love (1 John 4:8) but God is also holy — "This is the message which we have heard from Him and declare to you, that God is light and in Him is no darkness at all" (1 John 1:5, NKJV). God in His love did not desire that any of His creatures should have to perish[e], but to simply overlook our sins would deny His character of holiness. Most people, if they were to think about what God ought to be like, would expect Him to judge the perpetrators of atrocities and injustices that have been so frequently committed in the history of this world. They could not imagine a God that would simply pass over these matters. Indeed such terrible deeds will be judged[f], but if God is to deal with these things, He must also deal with every issue of *our* lives. God's standard is immeasurably higher than ours, and none of us can attain it[g]. God, in His infinite wisdom and love, has solved the problem by having another suffer the *righteous and full penalty* for *our* sins, so that all who will accept the fact that they are a sinner in the eyes of God, and need forgiveness, *can* be forgiven, in such a way as not to compromise either God's holiness or His love:

> "For when we were still without strength, in due time Christ died for the ungodly. For scarcely for a righteous man will one die; yet perhaps for a good man someone would even dare to die. But God demonstrates His own love toward us, in that while we were still sinners, Christ died for us. Much more then, having now been justified by His blood, we shall be saved from wrath through Him. For if when we were enemies we were reconciled to God through the death of His Son, much more, having been reconciled, we shall be saved by His life." (Romans 5:6-10, NKJV)

5. Bildad's first speech and Job's reply

JOB CHAPTERS 8 - 10

It is now Bildad's turn to speak, and he is more forcible than Eliphaz. Almost immediately he counsels Job to confess to God, so that his trial will be over (verses 5-7), and he also suggests that Job's children must have sinned since they have died (verse 4). What a terrible accusation! We know from Job chapter 1 that it was Satan who caused the death of Job's children. How careful we need to be before jumping to conclusions and seeing the judgement of God in the circumstances of others! This is illustrated in 1 Corinthians 11:17-34, where the Apostle Paul has to rebuke the Corinthians because of their abuse of the Lord's supper. Because of the gravity of what they were doing, God had been obliged to act in judgement, and some of their company were ill or had even died: "For this reason many *are* weak and sick among you, and many sleep"[a] (verse 30, NKJV). Note that Paul says *for this reason* many are weak, etc. — i.e. the judgement was because of the corporate sin, although it was apparently concentrated in individual persons. Those who were sick were not necessarily more culpable than the others.

We saw earlier that Eliphaz used his own experience in trying to reason with Job. Bildad uses the wisdom of the fathers (verses 8-10). "Let us look at what those who have gone before have found", he says; "we know very little, since we have been alive for such a short time, but our ancestors will teach us." Although it is not a bad starting place for any research, the 'wisdom of the fathers' is not an infallible basis! Firstly, the 'fathers' do not always agree. Furthermore, if "our days on earth are a shadow", so were theirs, so that they would not necessarily be better placed to understand than we[b].

Bildad then continues with illustrations from the natural world, and the main thrust of his argument is that the paths of those who forsake God lead to nothing. He then ends with a recommendation that Job should get right with God. Bildad, however, is no more able to convince Job than Eliphaz was. Job's response is given in chapter 9. He begins with a very important question: "Then Job answered and said: "Truly I know *it is* so, But how can a man be righteous before God?"" (verses 1-2, NKJV). It is probable that the thrust of Job's question was to refute Bildad's accusation — "You say that I must have sinned and should get right with God, but tell me: how could one ever be *really* right with Him?" The question of how we can be just with God needs careful consideration. To begin with, we can see how *not* to do this:

• The Lord Jesus said to the Pharisees "And He said to them, "**You are those who justify yourselves before men**, but God knows your hearts. For what is highly esteemed among men is an abomination in the sight of God" (Luke 16:15, NKJV; emphasis mine). There is no point justifying ourselves before, or comparing ourselves with, other men and women. It might make us feel good, but it will not do for God.

- In Luke 18:9-14, the Lord Jesus told a parable about a Pharisee and a tax collector who went to the temple to pray — the first to vaunt his supposed good deeds and character, and the second to confess his sins. In verse 14 the Lord says "I tell you, this man [i.e. the tax collector] went down to his house justified *rather* than the other [i.e. the Pharisee]; for everyone who exalts himself will be humbled, and he who humbles himself will be exalted." Presenting God with a long list of all our good deeds will not justify us.

- In Acts 13 the apostle Paul is speaking to Jews. He tells them that "and by Him everyone who believes is justified from all things **from which you could not be justified by the law of Moses**" (verse 39, NKJV; emphasis mine). Trying to keep God's laws, for example the ten commandments, will not justify us. We have the same comment in Romans 3:20: "Therefore by the deeds of the law no flesh will be justified in His sight, for by the law *is* the knowledge of sin."

- We see the way to be justified in Romans 3:24-28: **"being justified freely by His grace through the redemption that is in Christ Jesus**, whom God set forth *as* a propitiation by His blood, through faith, to demonstrate His righteousness, because in His forbearance God had passed over the sins that were previously committed, to demonstrate at the present time His righteousness, that He might be just and the justifier of the one who has faith in Jesus. Where *is* boasting then? It is excluded. By what law? Of works? No, but by the law of faith. **Therefore we conclude that a man is justified by faith apart from the deeds of the law**." (emphasis mine). There is a great deal to consider in this wonderful passage, but the main points can be summarised as follows:

1   <u>We are justified freely by grace</u> — we do not have to do anything of ourselves (and anyway we cannot), but God has had pity on us, and in His love He gives us freely what we need.

2   <u>It is through the redemption that is in Christ Jesus</u> — because the Lord Jesus has suffered the righteous penalty for our sins, we can be justified, in such a way that God can still be just while at the same time being the justifier of those sinners who now believe in Jesus.

3   <u>Finally, we are justified by faith</u> — we need to have faith in what Christ has done and in what God has said. We need to take God at His word if we are to benefit from His justification.

Returning to Job and his arguments, we see that he presents God as the all-powerful Sovereign, and he despairs of being able to be justified in His sight. "God can do anything" is the thrust of Job's argument: "God *is* wise in heart and mighty in strength. Who has hardened *himself* against Him and prospered" (verse 4). This is actually a very important principle. Ultimately, God can do anything, and all things *will* serve Him. But God does not want forced service. He wants us to be willing servants and worshippers. Given all that God has done for us, in sending His Son to die for our sins, and the glorious future which He has prepared for those who have been forgiven, it should not be difficult to want to worship God. It is never easy to submit ourselves to someone else, but if that someone else has shown and does show great love and great personal sacrifice on our behalf, then it is a different situation — it is now a question of our hearts being won for Him. "My son, give me your heart" is God's great desire (Proverbs 23:26, NKJV). Still, there will be those who continually resist God and reject His love. In a coming day they will be forced to acknowledge Him[c], but they will not enjoy God's favour — instead, they will be subjected to His anger[d].

Verses 5 - 11 show further the great power of God. It is interesting to compare this section with the account in Matthew 14:22-34. In the passage in Matthew we see one instance of the Lord's divinity shine through the veil of His humanity and humility. God, who "commands the sun, and it does not rise; He seals off the stars; He alone spreads out the heavens, And treads on the waves of the sea; He made the Bear, Orion, and the Pleiades, And the chambers of the south; He does great things past finding out, Yes, wonders without number" is seen on earth as Jesus of Nazareth, who also trod upon the waves of the sea, to the astonishment of His disciples.

"If He goes by me, I do not see *Him*; If He moves past, I do not perceive Him" was Job's complaint (verse 11). Job could see evidence of God's power in His creation, as he had just described, but he wanted to speak with God directly. We can arrive at some understanding of God from studying creation — "The heavens declare the glory of God; And the firmament shows His handiwork" (Psalm 19:1, NKJV) and "For since the creation of the world His [i.e. God's] invisible *attributes* are clearly seen, being understood by the things that are made, *even* His eternal power and Godhead, so that they are without excuse" (Romans 1:20, NKJV)[e]. However, we cannot get a *full* understanding of God simply through creation. How wonderful that God has now been fully revealed by the Lord Jesus Christ. John 1:18 tells us that "no one has seen God at any time" but goes on to say "The only begotten Son, who is in the bosom of the Father, He has declared *Him*." All that we need to know about God, His character, and His thoughts about us, have been fully revealed in Jesus Christ. We cannot therefore now say like Job that "if He goes by me, I do not see *Him*; If He moves past, I do not perceive Him".

Job however, at this stage in his experience, could only see with bitterness the apparent lack of concern of God. He sees God's great power but wonders why He does not act to help him: "For He crushes me with a tempest, And multiplies my wounds without cause. He will not allow me to catch my breath, But fills me with bitterness" (verses 17-18, NKJV). Job concludes that God must be acting in an arbitrary way: "It *is* all one *thing*; Therefore I say, 'He destroys the blameless and the wicked" (verse 22, NKJV) — in other words, "there does not seem to be any difference; both the good and the bad can end up in suffering". Not that this gives Job any comfort, as we see in verses 27-28: "If I say, 'I will forget my complaint, I will put off my sad face and wear a smile,' I am afraid of all my sufferings; I know that You will not hold me innocent." Once again Job wishes that he were able to speak with God directly, but he is afraid to do so: "For *He is* not a man, as I *am*, *That* I may answer Him, *And that* we should go to court together. Nor is there any mediator between us, *Who* may lay his hand on us both" (verses 32-33, NKJV).

Job is wanting someone to arbitrate, someone to plead his case for him before God. Job himself feels that he cannot approach God directly, so he wishes that there might be a 'mediator', who would have the right qualities, one who could approach God without fear, but also one who would understand Job's case. This mediator would thus be able to "lay his hand" on both God and Job, to use Job's illustration. But who would be able to perform such a function?

The New Testament supplies us with the answer to this. God, who wants us to be able to approach Him, yet fully understands our inability to stand before Him in our own merits, has provided the mediator that we need. 1 Timothy 2:5 tells us that "For *there is* one God and one Mediator between God and men, ***the* Man Christ Jesus**" (emphasis mine). We know from other passages in the Bible that Jesus Christ is God; He is God the Son[f]. Jesus is also a true Man, having been born in this world as a baby at Bethlehem. Here then is One who can fulfil this position of mediator between God and men: He is the Son of God, and so has perfect access to God the Father; He is also a Man, and so fully understands our case. Furthermore, He has fully satisfied all of God's requirements of holiness, since He has taken on Himself the penalty for our sins. The passage in 1 Timothy 2 goes on to say "who gave Himself a ransom for all, to be testified in due time" (verse 6, NKJV). This therefore is the way in which we can approach God — through our mediator Jesus Christ. This is why Jesus says "I am the way, the truth, and the life. No one comes to the Father except through Me" (John 14:6, NKJV).

Job could not know of this mediatorship, since Jesus Christ had not yet been revealed. In chapter 10 he expresses his bitterness, and at the same time justifies himself (verses 3 and 7). Once again he asks "Why did I live? Why was I brought forth?" (verses 18-22). And we see again Job's shadowy understanding of what lies beyond this life — to him it is a "land as dark as darkness *itself,* As the shadow of death". How fortunate we are to have the full revelation of the New Testament, in which is revealed our Mediator, the Lord Jesus Christ, and the certainty of something far better than a land of darkness and the shadow of death!

6. Zophar's first speech and Job's reply

JOB CHAPTERS 11 - 14

Zophar now takes up his argument against Job. As with Eliphaz and Bildad, *some true things are said*, but not necessarily *rightly applied*. Zophar begins by remonstrating with Job for his "multitude of words", and picks on Job's proclaimed self-righteousness: "For you have said, 'My doctrine *is* pure, And I am clean in your eyes.'" (verse 4). "I wish God would speak to you directly", is the thrust of his argument, "and then you would see how much of your evil He has overlooked, and how little you really know about Him!" (see verses 5-6). In fact, this is what God does, as we will see later on, when God speaks to Job out of the whirlwind. But it is only when God Himself speaks to us, through His Word, that our consciences are really touched and we see ourselves as we really are before Him. In the sight of His holiness, we realise what sinners we really are, but His love sustains us, as we realise too that God desires to justify us, and does so through the work of His Son, the Lord Jesus Christ[a]. The speeches of Eliphaz, Bildad and Zophar had the opposite effect — they led Job to cloak himself in more and more self-righteousness.

Zophar was right in saying that the secrets of God's wisdom are "the double of what is realised" (verse 6, J. N. Darby translation). In whatever field of study, whether it be deeper investigations into the natural world, or deeper study of the Word of God, how often we see further and further instances of God's great wisdom! "*It is* the glory of God to conceal a matter, But the glory of kings *is* to search out a matter." Proverbs 25:2, NKJV." (Proverbs 25:2, KJV). Zophar however felt that this meant that one could not find out God. Certainly, as creatures, we can never fully understand God (verse 7). Yet in the New Testament there is a wonderful answer to Zophar's statement in verses 7 - 8: "Can you search out the deep things of God? Can you find out the limits of the Almighty? *They are* higher than heaven—what can you do? Deeper than Sheol[b]—what can you know?" The answer is in the epistle to the Romans:

> "But the righteousness of faith speaks in this way, "Do not say in your heart, 'Who will ascend into heaven?'" (that is, to bring Christ down *from above*) or," 'Who will descend into the abyss?'" (that is, to bring Christ up from the dead). But what does it say? "The word is near you, in your mouth and in your heart" (that is, the word of faith which we preach): that if you confess with your mouth the Lord Jesus and believe in your heart that God has raised Him from the dead, you will be saved. For with the heart one believes unto righteousness, and with the mouth confession is made unto salvation. For the Scripture says, "Whoever believes on Him will not be put to shame."" (Romans 10:6-11, NKJV)

If it is true that we can never fully understand everything about God, so that figuratively such knowledge would be high as the heavens and deep as the grave, yet we do not need to ascend to such heights or descend to such depths to understand what we *need to know about God*. Such knowledge is not far away; it is not just for the learned; it is near us, and involves confessing the Lord Jesus Christ and believing in Him as a risen and living Saviour.

Zophar did not understand these things, but instead recommends that Job turn from his supposed evil ways, so as to find favour with God (verses 13 - 15). It is a very common thought, and evidently not a new one, that we can gain God's favour by doing good. There is a certain amount of truth in this *as far as this life is concerned*. Besides, we have the principle that we reap what we sow (Galatians 6:7). But we cannot gain God's favour simply by our supposed good deeds. We may be pretty good people when comparing ourselves to others, but we do not reach God's standards. Furthermore, no-one has ever been fully righteous before God, so there is always the question of past sins. "For all have sinned and fall short of the glory of God" (Romans 3:23, NKJV). The Bible therefore does not consider "doing good" as the opposite of "doing evil" where the subject of how to be right with God is concerned, contrary to what many believe. Rather, "doing evil" is contrasted with "doing truth" [9]. This is illustrated by John 3:19-21:

> "And this is the condemnation, that the light has come into the world, and men loved darkness rather than light, because their deeds were evil. "For every-one practicing evil hates the light and does not come to the light, lest his deeds should be exposed. "But he who does the truth comes to the light, that

his deeds may be clearly seen, that they have been done in God."

It is only in full light that we can properly see things as they are. In the full light of God's holiness, as shown to us by the life of Jesus Christ, we see our good deeds, and the motives behind them, as they really are. There are many who would prefer not to be subjected to this scrutiny, but rather to remain with the good opinion that they and others have of themselves. They are like those in the passage above who hate the light. But if we "do truth", i.e. by admitting what we really are in the sight of God, we will be justified, because God has provided forgiveness and justification for sinners.

Job replies to Zophar in chapter 12. In verses 1-5 we can see his exasperation with his friends. "No doubt you *are* the people, And wisdom will die with you! But I have understanding as well as you; I *am* not inferior to you. Indeed, who does not *know* such things as these?" (verses 2-3, NKJV). "It seems to me that you think you are the only wise people on the earth", Job is saying, "but I know at least as much as you!" It is never a good thing to pretend that we have all the answers when we are trying to help someone. None of us can fully appreciate the complexities of every situation, since our own experience and knowledge will necessarily be limited. We are far more likely to be listened to if we admit that we cannot explain everything, but instead we can point to One who can. Jesus Christ is our wisdom[c], and it is to Him that we can turn for every situation. We have a picture of the wisdom of Jesus Christ in the Old Testament, when the Queen of Sheba went to see King Solomon.

"Now when the queen of Sheba heard of the fame of Solomon concerning the name of the LORD, she came to test him with hard questions. She came to Jerusalem with a very great retinue, with camels that bore spices, very much gold, and precious stones; and when she came to Solomon, she spoke with him about all that was in her heart. So Solomon answered all her questions; there was nothing so difficult for the king that he could not explain *it* to her." (1 Kings 10:1-3, NKJV)

What Job's friends achieved by their lectures was to further entrench Job in his opinions. He justifies himself again in verse 4, and blames his friends for despising him while they were at ease in comfortable circumstances (verse 5). He then relates God's sovereign power in verses 7-25: power over the natural world, power over wise men and nobles, and power over nations. The implication, once again, is that God's power is seemingly used in an arbitrary way, such that the wicked may well be in easy circumstances (verse 6).

In chapter 13 Job again sharply criticises his friends. He calls them "forgers of lies" (verse 4), presumably because they have accused Job of being wicked, while he felt that he was just. He also refers to them as "worthless physicians" and wishes that they would keep silent rather than speak in the way that they have been (verse 5). Job's friends' intentions were no doubt kind when they decided to come and comfort Job (chapter 2 verses 11-13), but as we have seen, their analysis of the situation did little to help Job. Instead it brought out Job's bitterness and led to both sides exchanging harsh words. Sometimes it is wise to heed the advice of Proverbs 17:28 "Even a fool is counted wise when he holds his peace; *When* he shuts his lips, *he is considered* perceptive"!

Verses 13-16 are very interesting:

"Hold your peace with me, and let me speak, Then let come on me what *may*! Why do I take my flesh in my teeth, And put my life in my hands? Though He slay me, yet will I trust Him. Even so, I will defend my own ways before Him. He also *shall* be my salvation, For a hypocrite could not come before Him."

There is a great contrast here which gives us an insight to Job's faith. On the one hand he gives his expression to his bitterness: "Hold your peace with me, and let me speak, then let come on me what may", as much as to say, "I have suffered enough as it is, so I will say what I feel about it before God, and see what happens!" We have seen that Job felt that his sufferings were meted out to him in an arbitrary fashion, and this is the basis of his accusation of God. But then he says "Though He slay me, yet will I trust Him". It seems as if, in his heart, Job knows that God is not in fact acting in an arbitrary manner — even if God were to kill him, Job is sure that God is not ultimately against him. The tension between this deep, inner trust in God on the one hand, and his circumstances that seem to argue against trust in God, must have been extremely difficult for Job to cope with.

Job nevertheless continues to justify himself ("but I will defend mine own ways before him", verse 15b, J. N. Darby translation), and in verses 20-22 he desires to plead his cause with God. In verse 23 he asks "How many *are* my iniquities and sins? Make me know my transgression and my sin." This is an important question we can all ask ourselves: how many are *my* sins? If we compare ourselves to other people, we might delude ourselves into thinking that we are not that bad, or even pretty good people, leading a moral, upright life. It is when we compare ourselves to God's standard that we begin to realise our shortcomings. God has said plainly that "**all** have sinned and fall short of the glory of God" (Romans 3:23, NKJV; emphasis mine). The Lord Jesus Christ, when He was present on this earth, was the only person to have completely satisfied God with His life. At the beginning of His career, when He was baptised, God was able to say "This is My beloved Son, in whom I am well pleased" (Matthew 3:17, NKJV) and again in Matthew 17:5 at His transfiguration, there was "a voice [that] came out of the cloud, saying, "This is My beloved Son, in whom I am well pleased. Hear Him!"" He is the perfect example that defines God's standard. He is the only one who could say in truth and without any pride "for I always do those things that please Him" (John 8:29b, NKJV), and "Which of you convicts Me of sin?" (John 8:46a, NKJV). None of us can reach this standard, since we all have sins of commission (things we have done that we should not have done) and sins of omission (things we have not done that we should have done). We can therefore ask with Job "How many are my iniquities and sins?"

Thankfully the situation does not end there. Isaiah chapter 53 speaks prophetically of the forgiveness that the Lord Jesus Christ bought for us when He suffered the penalty of our sins on His cross.

> "Surely He has borne our griefs And carried our sorrows; Yet we esteemed Him stricken, Smitten by God, and afflicted. But He *was* wounded for our transgressions, *He was* bruised for our iniquities; The chastisement for our peace *was* upon Him, And by His stripes we are healed. All we like sheep have gone astray; We have turned, every one, to his own way; And the LORD has laid on Him the iniquity of us all. . . . Therefore I will divide Him a

portion with the great, And He shall divide the spoil with the strong, Because He poured out His soul unto death, And He was numbered with the transgressors, And He bore the sin of many, And made intercession for the transgressors." (Isaiah 53:4-6, 12, NKJV)

We will almost certainly never know the true number of our sins and iniquities before God, but if we have trusted in the Lord Jesus for His forgiveness, then we can be assured that He did know all of them, and suffered for all of them: past, present and future sins. If we know this to be true for ourselves, then we have no need to fear that God will "write bitter things against me, and make me inherit the iniquities of my youth" (Job 13:26, NKJV) — since all ours sins are forgiven, there is nothing left to be written down as a charge against us. "*There is* therefore now no condemnation to those who are in Christ Jesus" (Romans 8:1a, NKJV).

As Job continues his speech in chapter 14, he asks a number of most important questions. Firstly, although he has been justifying himself, he nevertheless realises that man is not pure before God: "Who can bring a clean man out of the unclean? Not one!" (verse 4, J. N. Darby translation). This agrees with several other passages in the Bible, that teach us that we are, in our very nature, unclean in God's sight. David acknowledged this in his Psalm of confession: "Behold, I was brought forth in iniquity, And in sin my mother conceived me." (Psalm 51:5, NKJV). The same truth is explained by the Apostle Paul: "Therefore, just as through one man sin entered the world, and death through sin, and thus death spread to all men, because all sinned . . . For as by one man's disobedience many were made sinners" (Romans 5:12 and 19a, NKJV). The Lord Jesus Himself had to explain this truth to Nicodemus, who was a prominent scholar of the Jewish religion. As we can read in John chapter 3, Nicodemus came by night to see the Lord Jesus. Jesus said to him "Most assuredly, I say to you, unless one is born again, he cannot see the kingdom of God" (John 3:3, NKJV). Nicodemus did not understand this, as we can see from his reply: "How can a man be born when he is old? Can he enter a second time into his mother's womb and be born?" (John 3:4, NKJV). Jesus therefore explained the situation again: "Most assuredly, I say to you, unless one is born of water and the Spirit, he cannot enter the kingdom of God. **That which is born of the flesh is flesh, and that which is born of the Spirit is spirit**. Do not marvel that I said to you, 'You must be born again.'" (John 3:5-7 NJV; emphasis mine). This is the central point: *that which is born of the flesh is flesh.* Whether it is refined or otherwise, educated or not, the flesh cannot be acceptable to God. Consequently, there is the absolute necessity for *new birth*. This is made possible by the forgiveness available through the Lord Jesus, and the regeneration of the Holy Spirit. It is not some esoteric teaching, but a simple reality, as the Lord Jesus further explained to Nicodemus:

> "For God so loved the world that He gave His only begotten Son, that whoever believes in Him should not perish but have everlasting life. For God did not send His Son into the world to condemn the world, but that the world through Him might be saved. He who believes in Him is not condemned; but he who does not believe is condemned already, because he has not believed in the name of the only begotten Son of God." (John 3:16-18, NKJV)

Job however did not have the clear understanding that we can have, through the revelation given to us in the New

Testament. In verses 5 - 6 he desires that God should leave him alone: "Since his days *are* determined, The number of his months *is* with You; You have appointed his limits, so that he cannot pass. Look away from him that he may rest, Till like a hired man he finishes his day." In other words, since the length of man's life is determined by God, and man in any case cannot be pure before God (verse 4), why cannot God just leave us alone until we die? But as we have just seen, God has thoughts of love towards us, and desires that we should take hold of the wonderful future that he wants us to have, and for which the Lord Jesus died on the cross, so that we could be brought into relationship with God. Far worse to be left alone by God, to remain in our sinful, unforgiven state! As an aside, it is indeed true that the length of our life is determined by God. The Lord Jesus says that He has the keys of death and Hades[d]. A comforting thought for those who have accepted His forgiveness, and thus know that there is only rest and true happiness beyond the grave. Their lives are in the complete control of a loving God, and even the moment of their death has been determined by Him, and cannot be altered by any other creature. But it is a solemn thing for those who are as yet "in their sins" — it would be dreadful to die in that state[e].

Job speaks of death (verses 10 - 12), and he seems to have had a vague idea of a future resurrection: "If a man dies, shall he live *again*? All the days of my hard service I will wait, Till my change comes" (verse 14, NKJV). But this thought does not entirely bring him peace: "Oh, that You would hide me in the grave, That You would conceal me until Your wrath is past, That You would appoint me a set time, and remember me!" (verse 13, NKJV). There are two important points to bring out here. The New

Testament tells us what is to come after death: "And as it is appointed for men to die once, **but after this the judgment**" (Hebrews 9:27, NKJV; emphasis mine). Death of the body does not mean death of the soul. Furthermore, the Bible teaches us clearly that there will be a resurrection of the body at a future date: "Do not marvel at this; for the hour is coming in which all who are in the graves will hear His voice and come forth—those who have done good, to the resurrection of life, and those who have done evil, to the resurrection of condemnation" (John 5:28-29, NKJV). Job desired that he might be hidden, so to speak, after his death, and that his resurrection ("my change") would occur once God's anger was past. But, as has been mentioned several times already, God's anger *is already past* for those who have trusted in the forgiveness available through the Lord Jesus. He suffered the judgement for our sins, as it is written: "For I delivered to you first of all that which I also received: that Christ died for our sins according to the Scriptures, and that He was buried, and that He rose again the third day according to the Scriptures" (1 Corinthians 15:3-4, NKJV) and again "who Himself [i.e. the Lord Jesus Christ] bore our sins in His own body on the tree, that we, having died to sins, might live for righteousness—by whose stripes you were healed" (1 Peter 2:24, NKJV). If we have accepted this forgiveness of our sins, then we can say with the Apostle Paul "*There is* therefore now **no condemnation** to those who are in Christ Jesus, who do not walk according to the flesh, but according to the Spirit" (Romans 8:1a, NKJV; emphasis mine). However, if we reject this offer of forgiveness, the latter half of John 3:36 will apply: "He who believes in the Son has everlasting life; and he who does not believe the Son shall not see life, but the wrath of God abides on him."

O Christ, what burdens bowed Thy head!
Our load was laid on Thee;
Thou stoodest in the sinner's stead
To bear all ill for me.
A victim led, Thy blood was shed;
Now there's no load for me.

Death and the curse were in our cup
O Christ, 'twas full for Thee!
But Thou hast drained the last dark drop,
'Tis empty now for me.
That bitter cup, love drank it up;
Left but the love for me.

Jehovah lifted up His rod
O Christ, it fell on Thee!
Thou wast forsaken of Thy God;
No distance now for me.
Thy blood beneath that rod has flowed:
Thy bruising healeth me.

The tempest's awful voice was heard,
O Christ, it broke on Thee;
Thine open bosom was my ward;
It bore the storm for me.
Thy form was scarred, Thy visage marred;
Now cloudless peace for me.

For me, Lord Jesus, Thou hast died,
And I have died in Thee;
Thou'rt risen: my bands are all untied;
And now Thou liv'st in me.
The Father's face of radiant grace
Shines now in light on me.

Mrs Anne Ross Cousin (1824 - 1906)

7. Eliphaz's second speech and Job's reply

JOB CHAPTERS 15 - 17

We now come to the start of the second cycle of speeches, in which Eliphaz, Bildad and Zophar in turn again argue with Job, and Job responds to each one. At first, Eliphaz had started off reasonably gently: "Then Eliphaz the Temanite answered and said: "*If* one attempts a word with you, will you become weary? But who can withhold himself from speaking?"" (Job 4:1-2, NKJV). Put another way, he had asked "Would you be upset if I had a talk with you — if I gave you some advice?" But now, Eliphaz is evidently irritated with Job's response that what he and his other two friends had said was not helpful. He accuses Job of unprofitable talk (verse 3), and then in verses 7-10, he is saying "Are you the wisest of men? Do you know everything? We know at least as much as you!" Verse 11 reads "*Are* the consolations of God too small for you, And the word *spoken* gently with you?" but the speeches of Job's three friends could hardly be classed as "words spoken gently" to him!

Eliphaz is also irritated by Job's protestations of innocence, and in verses 14 - 16 he asks how anyone who is a mere man could pretend to be pure — "man, *who is* abominable and filthy, Who drinks iniquity like water!" This is true, but thankfully, as we have seen, the Lord Jesus has taken up our cause.

Verses 17 - 18 show us that Eliphaz is basing himself on what he has seen and experienced, and what "the wise men" and "fathers" have said. While our own experience is a very valuable thing, it is not necessarily relevant to other people's situations. Besides, our own experiences are generally very subjective. For the all-important questions that Job was grappling with, *absolute truths and values* are needed, not subjective ones. In moral questions, and in things relating to the purpose of life and our relationship with and responsibility towards God, absolute values are needed. It is no good basing ourselves on relative values, on what has been handed down, or happens to be accepted by current society. Such things have no solid foundation. God has not left us alone in this regard, but we have His Word, given to us in the Bible, which explains us these things. That is why the Lord Jesus spoke of those who heard and did according to His words as builders constructing a house on solid rock — as opposed to those who ignored His words, and were like those who tried to build on sand (see Matthew 7:24-27).

The remainder of chapter 15 (verses 20 - 35) is taken up with a graphic description of the woes and torments of the wicked — with the clear implication that Job must be this type of person!

Job responds to Eliphaz in chapter 16. "I have heard many such things; Miserable comforters *are* you all!" he says in verse 2. Job's friends had laboured the point that he must be wicked, hence Job's feeling that he had already heard quite enough. In verses 4 – 5, Job goes on to say that he, too, could speak like they did if they were in his situation. But, says Job, "I would strengthen you with my mouth, And the comfort of my lips would relieve *your grief*" (verse 5, NKJV). In verse 10, Job's words remind us of what was said prophetically about the Lord Jesus on the cross. Job says "They gape at me with their mouth, They strike me reproachfully on the cheek, They gather together against me." Similarly, in Psalm 22, which speaks prophetically of the crucifixion of the Lord Jesus, we read in verse 13 "They gape at Me *with* their mouths". In the case of the Lord Jesus, His adversaries thought that He was being afflicted by God because of His own wrongdoing. Another prophetic passage, Isaiah 53:4 tells us "Surely He has borne our griefs And carried our sorrows; Yet we esteemed Him stricken, Smitten by God, and afflicted." The Lord Jesus had no sins of His own that He should be afflicted of God, but He was being afflicted for *our* sins, so that *we* could be forgiven. Job, on the other hand, was not perfect, yet God was not afflicting him for some specific sin, as his friends were suggesting, but rather that Job might learn some fundamental lessons about himself.

The problem was that the more Job's friends insisted that Job must be wicked to deserve all this suffering, the more Job justified himself and wrapped himself up in his own self-righteousness. Thus all were wrong: Job's friends were wrong in accusing Job unjustly, with no evidence that they could show to backup their claims, and Job was wrong in insisting that he was pure before God, and that therefore God must be acting unjustly and arbitrarily towards him. Job speaks of his sufferings and grief in verses 11 – 16, and in verse 17 he claims that he is pure: "Although no violence *is* in my hands, And my prayer *is* pure." He longs therefore for someone to mediate between God and himself: "Oh that there were arbitration for a man with God, as a son of man for his friend!" (verse 21, J.N. Darby's translation). Job had already expressed this desire in chapter 9 verse 33, and we considered this in chapter 5 of this commentary. As we have mentioned there already, the Lord Jesus is that mediator. He is often referred to as 'Son of Man' in the gospels, and so He is the true Son of Man that can be our friend and mediator between God and men, as Job desired to see. He is the one who was referred to as "a friend of tax collectors and sinners" (Luke 7:34b, NKJV). How wonderful that He was indeed willing to befriend us sinners, so that we might be brought into a relationship with God, with no fear of judgement!

Job, as yet, did not know these wonderful truths. We can know them readily, as we have the inestimable privilege of the complete Word of God, the Bible, easily available to us. We can therefore apply to ourselves the words that the Lord Jesus spoke to His disciples: "But blessed *are* your eyes for they see, and your ears for they hear; for assuredly, I say to you that many prophets and righteous *men* desired to see what you see, and did not see *it*, and to hear what you hear, and did not hear *it*" (Matthew 13:16-17, NKJV). If we have a great privilege, there is also a corresponding responsibility. In Matthew chapter 11, the Lord Jesus rebuked those cities in which He had performed His works of power, and yet many had not believed. The day of judgement would be more tolerable for Sodom, a city mentioned in the Old Testament that epitomised wickedness, than for Capernaum (verses 23-24). So we too, who have the opportunity to grasp the salvation offered to us by the Lord Jesus, will face severe judgement if this is refused. "Of how much worse punishment, do you suppose, will he be thought worthy who has trampled the Son of God underfoot, counted the blood of the covenant by which he was sanctified a common thing, and insulted the Spirit of grace? . . . It is a fearful thing to fall into the hands of the living God" (Hebrews 10:29, 31; NKJV).

In Job chapter 17, Job continues his speech by speaking of his sorrows, and complaining about his friends. "But please, come back again, all of you, For I shall not find *one* wise *man* among you" (verse 10, NKJV). In other words "You can keep up your speeches, but they are of no value to me." Unfortunately, the arguments between Job and his friends continued for some time, as we shall see in our following chapters. Unfortunately for Job, I say, in a sense, but fortunately for us. Every record in the Bible is for our profit[a], and we can gain many insights into the broader counsel of God, and His ways with us, even in these seemingly unending speeches!

8. Bildad's second speech and Job's reply

JOB CHAPTERS 18 - 19

Bildad, like Eliphaz earlier, was also irritated by Job's previous comments, as we see in Job 18:1-4. His pride was no doubt wounded, but this was no way to comfort a friend! In verse 4 he ends up being sarcastic: "You who tear yourself in anger, Shall the earth be forsaken for you? Or shall the rock be removed from its place?" In the remainder of the chapter, Bildad graphically describes the fate of the wicked man. Although Bildad was wrong in applying these words to Job, there are some true points that he makes. For example, in verses 7 – 9, he speaks about how the wicked end up being caught out in their own plans. "His own counsel casts him down" (verse 7b, NKJV) — by planning some wickedness, and trusting in his own intelligence, the wicked man ends up being destroyed by his own plans. A similar thought is given in Ezekiel chapter 28. Here, the King of Tyre is presented, and it is not difficult to see in him a picture of Satan. "Your heart was lifted up because of your beauty; You corrupted your wisdom for the sake of your splendor" (verse 17a, NKJV). Self-occupation, self-delight, and trusting in his own wisdom all led to the devil's downfall [3]. How different is the path of true wisdom: "The fear of the LORD *is* the beginning of knowledge" (Proverbs 1:7a, NKJV) and "Trust in the LORD with all your heart, And lean not on your own understanding; In all your ways acknowledge Him, And He shall direct your paths" (Proverbs 3:5-6, NKJV).

In verse 14, Bildad speaks of "the king of terrors", i.e. death. Satan uses the fear of death to keep men and women in bondage, as we read in Hebrews[a]. But if we have trusted the Lord Jesus, death is no more a "king of terrors", but rather becomes a gateway to life. Jesus' words in John 11:25 are "I am the resurrection and the life. He who believes in Me, though he may die, he shall live." So we can say "O Death, where *is* your sting? O Hades, where *is* your victory?" (1 Corinthians 15:55, NKJV).

Job answers Bildad in chapter 19. First of all, he complains that Bildad and his friends are crushing him, instead of comforting him: "How long will you torment my soul, And break me in pieces with words?" (verse 2, NKJV). Yet as Job points out in verse 4, all the while that they are insisting that Job must have sinned to deserve this trouble, they cannot specify what it is that he has done. Job therefore states in verse 6 that it is *God* who has overthrown him (J. N. Darby translation), as opposed to it being simply a punishment from God for a particular sin. He says in verse 11 that God is counting Job as one of His enemies. How far from the truth this actually was! Firstly, we see that it is those whom God *loves* that He chastens[b]. Furthermore, we are told what God's attitude towards us was when *we* were enemies towards Him: "For if when we were enemies we were reconciled to God through the death of His Son" (Romans 5:10a, NKJV) — in other words, while *we* were at enmity with God, *He* sent His

Son to die for our sins, so that we could be reconciled to Him[c].

Job continues his speech by telling of the pain of seeing friends and family forsake him (verses 13 - 19). The latter part of verse 20, "I have escaped by the skin of my teeth", has become proverbial. There are many phrases which have been taken from the Bible and are used in a current speech, though this is not often realised[d]. In verses 21-22 Job makes his pitiful plea: "Have pity on me, have pity on me, O you my friends, For the hand of God has struck me! Why do you persecute me as God *does*, And are not satisfied with my flesh?"[e] How sad to think that Job's friends, who had originally come to comfort him (Job 2:11) could now be so lacking in pity.

We then come to some beautiful verses, where we see Job's great faith, despite his lack of understanding. "For I know *that* my Redeemer lives, And He shall stand at last on the earth; And after my skin is destroyed, this *I know*, That in my flesh I shall see God, Whom I shall see for myself, And my eyes shall behold, and not another. *How* my heart yearns within me!" (verses 25 - 27, NKJV). Job had a certain hope of his Redeemer, and that he would see Him, even if he died physically. We saw earlier (chapter 6 of this commentary) that Job was able to say "Though He slay me, yet will I trust Him" (Job 13:15a, NKJV). We too, if we have been redeemed by the precious blood of the Lord Jesus Christ, can have that same certainty of seeing Him after this life is past. Contrast Job's hope with that of the wicked sorcerer Balaam, who had to say "I see Him, **but not now**; I behold Him, **but not near**" (Numbers 24:17a, NKJV; emphasis mine).

Finally, Job warned his friends that they, too, might well be the subject of God's anger once Job had been dealt with

THE GOSPEL IN JOB

(verses 28 - 29). This is in fact what did happen, as we shall see later on.

9. Zophar's second speech and Job's reply

JOB CHAPTERS 20 - 21

Job had said earlier "And if indeed I have erred, My error remains with me" (Job 19:4, NKJV). He was challenging his friends by saying that for all their suggestions that Job's wickedness had brought all this trouble on him, nevertheless they could not state what it was that he had done. In chapter 20 Zophar graphically describes the woes of the wicked, and in doing so implies that Job is guilty of greed and oppression. His vivid descriptions need little comment! Zophar prefaced his comments by saying "Therefore my anxious thoughts make me answer, Because of the turmoil within me. I have heard the rebuke that reproaches me, And the spirit of my understanding causes me to answer" (verses 2-3, NKJV). One does indeed get the impression that his tirade is the result of hasty speech, without too much forethought.

Job replies in chapter 21 to contradict Zophar's analysis. Thus, in verses 7-12, he says that the wicked often *do* appear to lead a settled and prosperous case. I would imagine that most readers of this commentary would agree — there have been many instances in history, and even today, when wicked men and women have *apparently* not been brought to justice, but rather have enjoyed the fruits of their oppression. I say *apparently*, for it is after death that accounts are settled. Verse 13 of our chapter is apt therefore: "They spend their days in wealth, And in a moment go down to the grave." As we read in the New Testament: "And as it is appointed for men to die once, **but after this the judgment**" (Hebrews 9:27, NKJV; emphasis mine). Thus the example of the rich man and Lazarus (Luke 16:19-31) is very relevant, as was mentioned in chapter 3 of this commentary.

Job goes on to say that because these wicked people have all that they desire in this life, they naturally do not want to know God or think about His ways. "Yet they say to God, 'Depart from us, For we do not desire the knowledge of Your ways. Who *is* the Almighty, that we should serve Him? And what profit do we have if we pray to Him?'" (verses 14-15, NKJV). There are many like this today. They are ignorant of their responsibility towards God, and God's thoughts about them, and they *do not want to know*. They would much rather not be bothered about such things; they do not see any benefit in serving God; on the contrary, their lifestyle seems to serve them very well. However, as Job points out, "their prosperity is not in their hand" (verse 16, NKJV). God will bring them into judgement — they are not the ultimate masters of their own lives and prosperity. But, as far as *man* can see, this judgement of God may not always be apparent (verses 23-26)[a].

Job concludes his response to Zophar by saying in effect "I know what you are thinking — you are saying 'where is the good man, and where is the wicked?' — but ask those around you: the wicked are reserved for the day of calamity" (see verses 27-30). Thus the 'comforts' of Job's friends were indeed in vain (verse 34).

In these two chapters we see a good example of hasty speech, from Zophar, which did nothing to comfort or help Job, and a very perceptive rebuttal by Job. We do not hear Zophar again — maybe he felt that there was nothing more to be said, or perhaps the fact that Job so clearly refuted his arguments left him unwilling to try again. Before we leave these two chapters and move onto the third cycle of arguments, it is worth weighing the truth of verses 32-33 of chapter 21: "Yet he shall be brought to the grave, And a vigil kept over the tomb. The clods of the valley shall be sweet to him; **Everyone shall follow him, As countless *have gone* before him**" (emphasis mine). An innumerable quantity of people have already passed into death, and every man and woman follows them, yet how many have given proper consideration to what lies beyond?

10. Eliphaz's third speech and Job's reply

JOB CHAPTERS 22 - 24

Eliphaz now starts off the third cycle of arguments. In the opening verses (22:1-4) he effectively says "God does not owe you anything, even if you are righteous". He is thus countering Job's claim that he was righteous by saying that this would not make God his debtor anyway. He then continues by actually charging Job with specific sins, as we shall see in the next verses. In one sense Eliphaz was right — God does not owe us anything; and if we live in a way which God requires, then we are simply fulfilling our duty[a]. We do not get a letter of congratulations from the police each time we keep to the speed limit when driving — we are expected to do so! However, God does not act in this way. Although He owes us nothing, He nevertheless delights to reward us when we please Him. He takes note of the times when we serve Him. God had spoken highly of Job when He confronted Satan: "Then the LORD said to Satan, "Have you considered My servant Job, that *there is* none like him on the earth, a blameless and upright man, one who fears God and shuns evil?""

(Job 1:8, NKJV). Notice the words *My servant Job*: God had affection for Job, and took delight in Him.

Eliphaz then forcibly accuses Job of many sins, in a completely unjustifiable manner: he claims that Job's iniquity is without end (verse 5), that he has been exacting towards the poor by taking their very clothes as surety, and has not helped the thirsty and starving (verses 6-7), but has favoured the wealthy instead of the widows and fatherless (verses 8-9). "Not surprisingly", Eliphaz says in effect, "you are now in all this trouble, Job!" (see verses 10-11). He then accuses Job of suggesting that God does not know, or does not concern Himself, with what is going on. "You say, 'How does God know?'" (see verse 13), "but the wicked men who were before the flood said the same, but this did not help them!" (see verses 15-17)[b].

Eliphaz's logical conclusion is that Job should reconcile himself to God: "Reconcile thyself now with him, and be at peace: thereby good shall come unto thee." (Job 22:21, J. N. Darby translation). "If you do this", Eliphaz is saying, "you will be in prosperity again" (see verses 22 - 30). No doubt this is good advice generally, that we should be reconciled to God. We know that God is holy, and that our sins and wrongdoings mean that we cannot stand before Him with a totally clear conscience. How then should we reconcile our differences? The answer is provided in the New Testament: "For if when we were enemies **we were reconciled to God through the death of His Son**, much more, having been reconciled, we shall be saved by His life" (Romans 5:10, NKJV; emphasis mine). As in all things, it is God who has taken the initiative, and we can be fully reconciled to Him, because His Son, the Lord Jesus Christ, died for our sins.

In chapter 23, Job takes up Eliphaz's comments, and replies in effect "Yes, I would willingly be reconciled to God, but where do I find Him? How can I get an audience with Him?" (see verses 1-3). It may be that many people have asked this sort of question, with more or less sincerity. They may have some conception that there is a God, to whom one day they will need to give an account for their lives, but where is He? How does one interact with Him? Once again, God has taken the initiative here — He has come to us. When the Lord Jesus came to this earth as a baby, it was said "Behold, the virgin shall be with child, and bear a Son, **and they shall call His name Immanuel, which is translated, "God with us"**" (Matthew 1:23, NKJV; emphasis mine). *Emmanuel* was one of the names given to the Lord Jesus, who came to make God known to us. All that we need to know, or indeed can know, about God has been fully made known to us in the Person of the Lord Jesus. On one occasion, His disciple Philip said "Lord, show us the Father, and it is sufficient for us" (John 14:8, NKJV), and the Lord Jesus had to reply "Have I been with you so long, and yet you have not known Me, Philip? He who has seen Me has seen the Father; so how can you say, 'Show us the Father'?" (John 14:9, NKJV). Furthermore, Jesus wanted men and women to come to Him, to find Him, so that they could be reconciled to God: "Come to Me, all *you* who labor and are heavy laden, and I will give you rest" (Matthew 11:28, NKJV). There is no risk of being rejected: "the one who comes to Me I will by no means cast out" (John 6:37b, NKJV). Sadly, however, He had to say of some **"But you are not willing to come to Me** that you may have life" (John 5:40, NKJV; emphasis mine). God has come very close to each one of us; He wants us to come to Him, but He will not force us. There are some who will reject His love, and will have to suffer the consequences of their own choice.

Job continues his speech in verses 4-7. "If I could find Him", he is saying, "then I could meet with God, reason with Him, and justify myself. He would understand my case." Job needed to learn that, while he was no doubt not guilty of the particular sins that Eliphaz had charged him with, yet he could not possibly stand before God in his *own* merits. He did not appreciate God's holiness and his own sinfulness. It is a very common mistake! We are all prone to compare ourselves with others, generally those whom we think are much worse than ourselves, and we feel that we are pretty good, honest people! But the standard of God's holiness is a dreadfully high one. Who of us could honestly say that we have always attained the standard outlined by the Lord Jesus in the 'sermon on the mount' (see Matthew chapters 5-7)? In Isaiah chapter 6, the prophet Isaiah speaks of a vision that he had, when he was brought into the presence of God. Isaiah was doubtless a godly man, and we do not hear anything in the Bible that tells us of failings or sins on his part. Nevertheless, he did not feel at ease in God's presence:

"In the year that King Uzziah died, I saw the Lord sitting on a throne, high and lifted up, and the train of His *robe* filled the temple. Above it stood seraphim; each one had six wings: with two he covered his face, with two he covered his feet, and with two he flew. And one cried to another and said: "Holy, holy, holy *is* the LORD of hosts; The whole earth *is* full of His glory!" And the posts of the door were shaken by the voice of him who cried out, and the house was filled with smoke. So I said: "Woe *is* me, for I am undone! Because I *am* a man of unclean lips, And I dwell in the midst of a people of unclean lips; For my eyes have seen the King, The LORD of hosts." Then one of the seraphim flew to me, having in his hand a live coal *which* he had taken with the tongs from the altar. And he touched my mouth *with it*, and said: "Behold, this has touched your lips; Your iniquity is taken away, And your sin purged." (Isaiah 6:1-7, NKJV).

In the presence of the Holy God Himself, Isaiah felt keenly his own unfitness to be there. "Woe is me, for I am undone, because I am a man of unclean lips", was his own confession. Even though we have no particular reason to believe that Isaiah was a very sinful man, he immediately felt the 'uncleanness' of his lips. This is perhaps not too surprising — we all, no doubt, often offend in what we say. How difficult it is never to speak badly of others, behind their backs, to gossip, to say unkind things when we are provoked, and so on. Changing the metaphor from lips to tongue, the Bible tells us in James chapter 3 verses 7-9: "For every kind of beast and bird, of reptile and creature of the sea, is tamed and has been tamed by mankind. But no man can tame the tongue. *It is* an unruly evil, full of deadly poison. With it we bless our God and Father, and with it we curse men, who have been made in the similitude of God." How true, therefore, that "if anyone does not stumble in word, he *is* a perfect man" (James 3:2, NKJV)!

What should Job do, then, and what should we do, if to stand in the presence of God so clearly demonstrates our unfitness in *His* sight, because of His holiness? We can turn to Isaiah again for the answer, as in his book he records God's comments on the matter: "Come now, and let us reason together," Says the LORD, "Though your sins are like scarlet, They shall be as white as snow; Though they are red like crimson, They shall be as wool" (Isaiah

1:18, NKJV). God *does* want us to meet with Him: He wants us to admit our sinfulness, for then He is able to justify us. Even though our sins may stand out like scarlet or crimson stains, they can be blotted out completely.

Job however had not yet understood these things. In verses 10-12 of chapter 23 he protests his innocence and integrity, and in verse 13 he accuses God of acting in an arbitrary way: "But he is in one *mind*, and who can turn him? And what his soul desireth, that will he do" (J.N. Darby translation). God can indeed do anything, but He does not do things arbitrarily — He will always remain true to His character of holiness and love.

Nevertheless, Job was not guilty of the sins that Eliphaz accused him of in chapter 22 verses 5-9. In chapter 24, Job contradicts Eliphaz to point out that those guilty of crimes and oppression often *do* appear to succeed in this life — but not ultimately (see verses 19-20 and 23-24). Once again, then, Eliphaz did not succeed in helping Job, but rather we see Job and his friends becoming more and more entrenched in their positions. In the next chapter we have the final comment from Job's friends, viz. the third speech of Bildad, and Job's response, after which Job's friends run out of arguments!

11. Bildad's third speech and Job's reply

JOB CHAPTERS 25 - 31

Bildad replies to Job for the last time, and his speech is short and sharp — just six verses. The thrust of his argument is simple: Job had justified himself in his previous reply to Eliphaz, but Bildad asks how anyone could possibly be pure in God's sight.

Job was clearly unimpressed with this argument (chapter 26 verses 1-4). He then goes on to speak of the power of God in creation (verses 5-14). It is worth noticing in passing the reference to God "hanging the earth on nothing" (verse 7). Evidently men such as Job had a better understanding of the universe than is sometimes thought. The Bible and 'modern' science are not incompatible, as some assert: clearly the Creator is the best Person to describe His creation! However, impressive as the natural world and the universe are, they do not give us a full revelation of God. Job acknowledges this in verse 14: "Indeed these *are* the mere edges of His ways, And how small a whisper we hear of Him! But the thunder of His power who can understand?" The creation speaks eloquently of the power of the Creator, but what is He like? How will He be disposed towards us? Are we important in His sight? Such questions as these need a further revelation of God if they are to be answered. Only if God is willing to reveal more of Himself to us can we know anything of His character and how He thinks about us. How wonderful, then, that Jesus Christ, the Son of God, condescended to come to this earth in human flesh, so that we might be able to know God in a way that we could understand.

Job did not yet fully understand the character of God — both His holiness and His love. In chapter 27 verses 1-6, Job again maintains that he is righteous, and that he has done nothing wrong. "Far be it from me That I should say you are right;" he says to his friends, "Till I die I will not put away my integrity from me. My righteousness I hold fast, and will not let it go; My heart shall not reproach *me* as long as I live." The logical conclusion, then, in Job's mind, is that God "has taken away my justice, ... [and] made my soul bitter" (verse 2, NKJV). Job has yet to learn, as we all need to learn, that whereas we may not be guilty of gross *outward* sins, as Job's friends were accusing him of, yet we are not pure before God's sight. We do not have any 'right' before God; rather we come under the sentence that "the wages of sin is death" (Romans 6:23, NKJV). Nevertheless, God does not want us to receive this wage. He desires to justify us, but not because of our own righteousness, but because the Lord Jesus Christ has paid the penalty for our sins, and we can come into the good of *His* righteousness. The Apostle Paul stated that he desired to be "not having my own righteousness, which *is* from the law, but that which *is* through faith in Christ, the righteousness which is from God by faith" (Philippians 3:9, NKJV). He realised that his own righteousness could only be tarnished, as it would depend upon having at all times fulfilled God's law in every way. There has only ever be one Person who has done this, the Lord Jesus Christ, but we can be considered as righteous in Him — altogether a far superior option.

Job then returns to one of his favourite themes (chapter 27 verses 8-23): the wicked may appear to succeed, but will eventually be judged. The wicked man has no future. Job emphasises these points to his friends: "Surely all of you have seen *it*; Why then do you behave with complete nonsense?" (verse 12, NKJV). He seems to be saying "Look, you keep insisting that I must have committed some dreadful sin since God has brought me into this terrible condition. But as I keep trying to tell you, those who do commit terrible sins often appear to be successful, even though eventually they will be called to account. I, on the other hand, am pure."

In chapter 28 Job becomes more philosophical, and muses about wisdom. We have an interesting description of mining for precious ores and stones in verses 1-11, but Job's point is that this is not how wisdom is found (verse 12). Wisdom is worth more than gold and precious stones (verses 15-19), and therefore the search and effort to mine these natural substances cannot compare with the need to find wisdom. But what is it, and where can it be found? — "Man does not know its value, Nor is it found in the land of the living. The deep says, '*It is* not in me'; And the sea says, '*It is* not with me.' ... From where then does wisdom come? And where *is* the place of understanding?" (Job 28:13-14, 20; NKJV).

Where indeed? "Destruction and Death say, 'We have heard a report about it with our ears'" (Job 28:22; NKJV). This is, at first sight, a somewhat obscure verse. But does it not suggest that death, with all that it entails, has something to say about the subject of wisdom? If this life is all there is, then to find a meaning for life, and an understanding of what true wisdom is, will be an impossible task. Yet there is something within us that rebels against the thought that this life is pointless and devoid of meaning, and that death abolishes all. Why do we have this thirst for wisdom, and why does the forbidding presence of death leave so many questions unanswered?

The answers are found with God: "God understands its way, And He knows its place" (Job 28:23; NKJV). God will make us know the truth about wisdom: "And to man He said, 'Behold, the fear of the Lord, that *is* wisdom, And to depart from evil *is* understanding'" (Job 28:28, NKJV). This is quoted in the book of wisdom, the Proverbs: "The fear of the LORD *is* the beginning of knowledge, *But* fools despise wisdom and instruction" (Proverbs 1:7; NKJV). An acknowledgement of God, a desire to please Him and to be right with Him; here is the "beginning of wisdom". God will ensure that such a quest will not remain unanswered: "for the same Lord over all is rich to all who call upon Him" (Romans 10:12; NKJV); "For You, Lord, *are* good, and ready to forgive, And abundant in mercy to all those who call upon You" (Psalm 86:5; NKJV). Compare this with the symbolical description of the sin and fall of the one now known as Satan, in Ezekiel 28:11-19, where he is represented as the 'King of Tyre'. Verse 17 speaks of him as follows: "Your heart was lifted up because of your beauty; You corrupted your wisdom for the sake of your splendor". Here was no "fear of the Lord", which is the beginning of wisdom, but a proud self-occupation and self-interest, with the result that his wisdom became corrupted [3].

Job continues his speech in chapter 29. We have a description of his former days, and the impression is clearly given that Job was indeed a righteous man, who looked after the interests of the poor and needy, and that he possessed and enjoyed great respect among his contemporaries. He had a place of honour that he clearly delighted in. What a contrast we have in chapter 30! The place of honour has disappeared, and Job is no longer respected. We may wonder whether Job had been slightly proud, during his period of prosperity, when we read verse 1 of chapter 30: "But now they mock at me, *men* younger than I, Whose fathers I disdained to put with the dogs of my flock." These outcasts, who are graphically described in verses 1-14, are now despising Job, since they see that God has (apparently) cast off Job: "*They were* sons of fools, Yes, sons of vile men; They were scourged from the land. And now I am their taunting song; Yes, I am their byword. They abhor me, they keep far from me; They do not hesitate to spit in my face. Because He has loosed my bowstring and afflicted me, They have cast off restraint before me" (Job 30:8-11, NKJV).

To be fair to Job, it is only too easy to be pleased with oneself when in prosperity, especially if we are recognised as those who do good and help others. It is pleasing to the natural heart to be wealthy enough to be in comfortable circumstances, while also to have the approbation of our own conscience and of our contemporaries as we help others out. Not that being rich or doing good is wrong in itself, I hasten to add! Indeed, the New Testament teaches "Command those who are rich in this present age not to be haughty, nor to trust in uncertain riches but in the living God, who gives us richly all things to enjoy. *Let them* do good, that they be rich in good works, ready to give, willing to share" (1 Timothy 6:17-18, NKJV). But how difficult it is not to be haughty, not to have proud or self-satisfied thoughts about ourselves! How remarkable, then, to consider the Lord Jesus Christ, the Creator and Sovereign of the universe, as described in the epistle to the Philippians: "Let this mind be in you which was also in Christ Jesus, who, being in the form of God, did not consider it robbery to be equal with God, **but made Himself of no reputation**, taking the form of a bondservant, *and* coming in the likeness of men" (Philippians 2:5-7, NKJV; emphasis mine).

Job, far from enjoying his former prosperity, was suffering much from his affliction: verses 15-19 describe the symptoms of his disease. Job charges God as having become cruel towards him (verse 21), and that prayer is useless: "Indeed, no prayer availeth when he stretcheth out his hand: though they cry when he destroyeth." (Job 30:24, J. N. Darby translation).

From verse 25 of chapter 30, and in all of chapter 31, Job maintains his righteousness. He lists out his good deeds, which would, no doubt, put many of us to shame, and he thus clearly rebuffs the accusations of Eliphaz, Bildad and Zophar, who had tried to prove that Job must have been a wicked man to deserve the trouble that had come upon him. Clearly, Job was not a wicked man. God Himself recognised this, as we saw at the beginning of this study: "Then the LORD said to Satan, "Have you considered My servant Job, that *there is* none like him on the earth, a blameless and upright man, one who fears God and shuns evil?"" (Job 1:8, NKJV). Satan had thought that Job would curse God if God allowed evil circumstances to come upon Job, and God had allowed Satan to afflict him. As we saw, Satan wasted no time in his malicious work against Job. Yet not once did Job curse God. In fact, we have no record of Job complaining, until his three friends came to 'comfort' him. Their misguided efforts, and incorrect analyses, did nothing to help Job. In spite of all of these circumstances, i.e. Satan's wickedness and the insensitivity and incompetence of Job's friends, God was using the events to teach Job a valuable lesson, as we shall see. Job needed to learn not to trust in his own self-righteousness. The attacks of his friends only served to further confirm Job in his self-righteous thoughts. Something better was needed to bring Job to an understanding of things as they really were. We shall see this in the following chapters.

12. Elihu and his speech

JOB CHAPTERS 32 - 37

Someone new now appears on the scene — Elihu, whose name means 'God (or whose God) is He' (note in J.N. Darby's translation of the Bible). For convenience, I have divided Elihu's speeches into the following sections:

• Job chapter 32 — Introduction and summary of the situation so far.

• Job chapter 33 — Elihu's first speech to Job, starting with the words *But please, Job, hear my speech, And listen to all my words* (verse 1). The true purpose of God's ways are brought out.

• Job chapter 34 — Elihu's second speech, starting with the words *Elihu further answered and said* (verse 1). Elihu justifies God and His actions.

• Job chapter 35 — Elihu's third speech, starting with the words *Moreover Elihu answered and said* (verse 1). Elihu opposes Job's self-righteousness.

• Job chapter 36:1-21 — Elihu's fourth speech, starting with the words *Elihu also proceeded and said* (verse 1).

Elihu further justifies God, and again states His true purpose in discipline.

• Job chapter 36:22 to end of chapter 37 — Elihu continues his fourth speech with the words *Behold, God is exalted by His power; Who teaches like Him?* (verse 22) and speaks of God's great power.

JOB CHAPTER 32 — INTRODUCTION

We now have Elihu brought before us, although there was no mention of him previously. The context of verses 1-5 shows that Elihu was present all the time with Eliphaz, Bildad and Zophar, and it is possible that Elihu himself may have written part or all of the book of Job, since in verses 15-16 it seems as if he is narrating: "They are dismayed and answer no more; Words escape them. And I have waited, because they did not speak, Because they stood still *and* answered no more."

One of the first things that comes across is that Elihu is *spiritually intelligent* [8]: very quickly he summarises the whole issue, and then proceeds with worthwhile things to say. It is quite a change from Eliphaz, Bildad and Zophar, who were not helpful, even though they did say some true things, yet not necessarily applied in the right manner. Firstly, we are told that Elihu was angered because on the one hand Job was justifying himself rather than God (verse 2), and on the other hand Job's friends were accusing Job without having any grounds to do so (verse 3). This pretty well summarises the previous 28 chapters! However, although Elihu was evidently bursting to speak (see verses 18-20), he had waited patiently because Job and his other friends were older than he was. This is a very commendable attitude, and shows that in spiritual things, as in other matters, *self-control* is a valuable asset. We have similar instructions in the New Testament, where the

Apostle Paul is speaking about the proper order that should characterise the church: "And the spirits of the prophets are subject to the prophets. For God is not *the author* of confusion but of peace, as in all the churches of the saints" (1 Corinthians 14:32-33, NKJV).

Elihu says in verses 6-9 that one might expect the aged to have greater wisdom, but it is not always so. Certainly in matters to do with God, age is of far less consequence than *spiritual intelligence*. Elihu alludes to this in verse 8: "But *there is* a spirit in man, And the breath of the Almighty gives him understanding." It is the presence of the Holy Spirit that gives us the ability to understand God and His ways. The Apostle Paul speaks about this very clearly in the following passage:

> "But as it is written: "Eye has not seen, nor ear heard, Nor have entered into the heart of man The things which God has prepared for those who love Him." But God has revealed *them* to us through His Spirit. For the Spirit searches all things, yes, the deep things of God. For what man knows the things of a man except the spirit of the man which is in him? Even so no one knows the things of God except the Spirit of God. Now we have received, not the spirit of the world, but the Spirit who is from God, that we might know the things that have been freely given to us by God. These things we also speak, not in words which man's wisdom teaches but which the Holy Spirit teaches, comparing spiritual things with spiritual. But the natural man does not receive the things of the Spirit of God, for they are foolishness to him; nor can he know *them*, because they are spiritually discerned. But he who is spiritual judges all things, yet he himself is *rightly* judged by no one. For "who has known the mind of

the LORD that he may instruct Him?" But we have the mind of Christ." (1 Corinthians 2:9-16, NKJV).

It is clear from the passage quoted above that the 'natural man', i.e. an unconverted person who does not have the Spirit of God, is not able to enter into an understanding of God's ways. Nevertheless, the Holy Spirit can work on such a person, to bring him to a realisation of his guilty state before God, and his need of forgiveness. If he believes and receives this, then he will be converted, and the Holy Spirit will give him spiritual life: "In Him you also *trusted*, after you heard the word of truth, the gospel of your salvation; **in whom also, having believed, you were sealed with the Holy Spirit of promise**" (Ephesians 1:13, NKJV; emphasis mine).

In many ways, Elihu illustrates how the Holy Spirit works with various individuals, as we shall see in the following sections. We can see this in verses 12-13, where Elihu states that none of Job's friends were able to convince Job, but that it would be God, not man, who would make Job yield. If someone is going to be convinced of their guilty state before God and their need of forgiveness, it must be through the work of God's Spirit. He may use other people, books, etc., but ultimately it is God's Word, in the power of the Holy Spirit, that will do the work. God's Word is always true — it does not adapt itself to what we might like to hear, or political correctness, for example. Similarly, Elihu states at the outset (verses 21-22) that he will not be flattering anyone, but rather speaking the truth, and explaining things as they really are.

JOB CHAPTER 33 — THE PURPOSE OF GOD'S WAYS

Job chapter 33 is a particularly interesting chapter as it shows clearly the true purpose of the ways of God, and how He works to bring us to forgiveness and relationship with Himself. Elihu starts off in verses 1-7 by taking a humble position; he acknowledges that *he himself* is nothing, and *in himself* is no better than Job: "Behold, before God I am as thou; I also am formed out of the clay." (Job 33:6, J. N. Darby translation). However, or perhaps as a consequence of this, his words are with authority, no doubt because they are *spiritual*. In matters of life and death, God, judgement and forgiveness, heaven and hell, it is vital to be able to speak *authoritatively*, i.e. to know what one is speaking about, and to be certain that it is the truth. The Lord Jesus did this when He was on this earth: "And so it was, when Jesus had ended these sayings, that the people were astonished at His teaching, for He taught them as one having authority, and not as the scribes" (Matthew 7:28-29, NKJV).

Elihu continues with a succinct and accurate statement of Job's position (verses 8-11). Basically, Job was claiming that he was pure and totally without fault, and yet God was unjustly afflicting him, and treating Job as an enemy. Elihu's response to this can initially seem surprising: "Look, *in* this you are not righteous. I will answer you, For God is greater than man. Why do you contend with Him? For He does not give an accounting of any of His words" (Job 33:12-13, NKJV). Rather than starting by disagreeing with Job's comments, Elihu simply says in effect "You are wrong to question God — it is not your place to do so, and God does not have to justify His actions to you." God does in fact have excellent reasons for acting as He does, and they are for our benefit, as Elihu will show, so why does Elihu start off with this rather unpalatable statement? I think the reason is that we need to recognise our position as creatures before God; to have the right attitude at the outset, before He can bless us. We are told that "God resists the proud, But gives grace to the humble" (James 4:6b, NKJV; see also 1 Peter 5:5, and Proverbs 3:34, which is the source of these quotations). In very similar fashion, the Apostle Paul replies to a question in Romans 9:19-20: "You will say to me then, "Why does He still find fault? For who has resisted His will?" But indeed, O man, who are you to reply against God? Will the thing formed say to him who formed *it*, "Why have you made me like this?"" We cannot simply go to God on our own terms; we need to recognise His sovereignty.

However, straight after this seemingly hard answer, Elihu continues with a wonderful presentation of the gospel in verses 14-34. We can consider an outline of this passage as follows. God speaks to men and women more than once, but we do not always listen or understand (v. 14), often because *pride* is our biggest problem (v. 17). If we are not listening to God, He may need to 'speak louder' by means of unpleasant circumstances (vs. 19-22). God wants to bring us to our senses by this discipline, to teach us about the fundamental, all-important issues of life. No doubt He would prefer not to have to afflict us if we would listen in the first place, but sometimes it is only difficult circumstances that will drive us to God and tear us away from the thousands of distractions that surround us. A *messenger* is required to help us make sense of all these things (v. 23). It would seem that they are rare — "one among a thousand" — but God is in control of all things, and will send one to those who are in need. We can praise God that He does send them, but if we are in a living relationship with Him, we could desire also to be such a messenger. The messenger comes with good news: You will not be going to the grave and to the destroyers (v. 22), because a ransom has been found for you! (v. 24). This is the central message of the gospel of God's grace: *a ransom has been found*. The true ransom, that answers to the picture given here by Elihu, is the Lord Jesus Himself. We are told plainly in the New Testament that He carried "our sins in His own body on the tree [i.e. the cross], that we, having died to sins, might live for righteousness—by whose stripes you were healed" (1 Peter 2:24, NKJV). If we accept this, we will never have to suffer the consequences of our sins after death, because the Lord Jesus was our ransom, and justice has already been exacted.

The wonderful truth of a ransom found is further pictured in verses 27-28 by Elihu. Verse 27 states "Then he looks at men and says, 'I have sinned, and perverted *what was* right, And it did not profit me.'" This again is the central message of the gospel, if we will accept it: *we* have sinned, but it will not be a charge against us. Verses 29-30 show us that this is what God desires, and wishes to make us understand. It is a wonderful thing when we have the assurance that our sins *are* forgiven, and that all judgement is passed. We can join in the following sentiment:

> *In Him I dare be joyful, a hero in the war,*
> *The judgement of the sinner affrighteth me no more.*
> *There is no condemnation, there is no hell for me,*
> *The torment and the fire my eyes shall never see;*
> *For me there is no sentence, for me death has no stings,*
> *Because the Lord Who saved me shall shield me with His*
> *wings.*

> Paul Gerhardt († 1676),
> translated by Mrs Emma Frances Bevan.

JOB CHAPTER 34 — ELIHU JUSTIFIES GOD AND HIS WAYS

Having explained the underlying purpose of God's ways, which is to bless, Elihu justifies God and rebukes Job for having suggested that God was acting unfairly and unjustly towards him: "For Job has said, 'I am righteous, But God has taken away my justice'" (verse 5, NKJV). And as a corollary to this, Job was saying that there was no point in being righteous before God, since evil circumstances would occur anyway! (see verse 9). Elihu indignantly refutes this: "Therefore listen to me, you men of understanding: Far be it from God *to do* wickedness, And *from* the Almighty to *commit* iniquity" (verse 10, NKJV). It is totally foreign to God's character to do evil, Elihu states, and besides, who are we to take God to task for what He does? — He is the owner of the world, and He is answerable to no-one (verses 12-13). If He wanted to, Elihu continues, He could simply think of Himself and dispose of us all: "If he only thought of himself, and gathered unto him his spirit and his breath, All flesh would expire together, and man would return to the dust" (verses 14-15, J.N. Darby's translation). However, this is not the case; God does think of us, and is completely impartial — He is "most just" (verse 17). As such, He is fully aware of all our doings, even if others are not (verse 21); we cannot hide from Him (verse 22), which is a solemn thought.

JOB CHAPTER 35 — ELIHU OPPOSES JOB'S SELF-RIGHT-EOUSNESS

Job had not only criticised God and His ways (see section above), but was thereby implicitly stating that *he* was more righteous than God was! (verse 2). In his bitterness, Job had asked what was the point of trying to be righteous — he might just as well have been wicked (verse 3). Yes,

Elihu replies, in one sense what you do does not appear to affect God, although it may affect other people (see verses 5-8)[a]. But the point is that God *is* concerned about people and their actions, yet none seek after Him (verse 10). God teaches us more than the beasts of the earth — unlike the animals, we have the opportunity to be in relationship with God (verse 11).

JOB CHAPTER 36:1-21 — ELIHU FURTHER JUSTIFIES GOD

Elihu continues his speech to speak about the ways of God. In verse 5 he tells us that although God is mighty, He does not despise us. He disciplines us so that we might recognise our iniquity, and be forgiven and restored (verses 10-12). However, the "hypocrites in heart" refuse to acknowledge this, and consequently they heap up anger towards themselves (verse 13). The Apostle Paul says the same thing in the New Testament: "Or do you despise the riches of His goodness, forbearance, and longsuffering, not knowing that the goodness of God leads you to repentance? But in accordance with your hardness and your impenitent heart you are treasuring up for yourself wrath in the day of wrath and revelation of the righteous judgment of God" (Romans 2:4-5, NKJV). For people such as this, it is not wise to "desire the night" and "be cut off": get right with God first! (verse 20).

JOB CHAPTER 36:22 - END OF CHAPTER 37 — THE POWER OF GOD

Elihu now speaks of the power of God in creating and sustaining the world. The basic message appears to be that God is a wise and powerful Creator and Sovereign, who controls the whole workings of nature perfectly. As such He should be respected, and also trusted — the One who so wonderfully controls the natural world will surely be in control of Job's situation. Chapter 36 verses 24-26 remind us "Remember to magnify His work, Of which men have sung. Everyone has seen it; Man looks on *it* from afar. Behold, God *is* great, and we do not know *Him*; Nor can the number of His years *be* discovered." These verses speak to us about some fundamental points: (1) we should give God the glory for what He has done, both in creation and redemption, (2) His works of creation can be clearly seen by all, and (3) although we cannot derive complete knowledge of God from His creation alone, His greatness is clearly evident.

Of course these days the theory of evolution is prevalent throughout the Western world, and it is probably fair to say that popular opinion is that science and evolution have replaced the need for God to explain why we are here in this world. It is beyond the scope of this commentary to enter into the creation/evolution debate. Suffice it to say that intelligent design is clearly stamped on all aspects of the natural world and universe. This is particularly evident in the realms of biology and biochemistry, where we have a magnificent system of coded information in the form of nucleic acids (e.g. DNA) which unify all life-forms, and the intricate biochemical pathways that underlie all biological functions. For those readers who are interested in serious information on these issues, the following references will prove useful [6, 7].

One does not need to be a scientist, however, to see the evidence of God's creation. As mentioned above, the hallmark of intelligent design is obvious. The Bible does not offer proof that God is creator — this is deemed to be self-evident, and therefore *an acknowledgement of this is a responsibility*. This puts the whole subject on a more solemn footing than a mere academic argument between creationists and evolutionists, however interesting and necessary this is[b]. We can see this from two quotations, one from the Old Testament, and one from the New:

"The heavens declare the glory of God; and the expanse sheweth the work of his hands. Day unto day uttereth speech, and night unto night sheweth knowledge. There is no speech and there are no words, yet their voice is heard. Their line is gone out through all the earth, and their language to the extremity of the world" (Psalm 19:1-4a, J. N. Darby translation).

In the above quotation, the heavens (i.e. stars, planets etc.) are said to declare the glory of God. This is a clear message — there are no words as such, yet throughout all the earth, this message of God's creatorial greatness can be clearly seen. In the New Testament, the Apostle Paul takes up a similar theme:

"For the wrath of God is revealed from heaven against all ungodliness and unrighteousness of men, who suppress the truth in unrighteousness, because what may be known of God is manifest in them, for God has shown *it* to them. For since the creation of the world His invisible *attributes* are clearly seen, being understood by the things that are made, *even* His eternal power and Godhead, so that they are without excuse, because, although they knew God, they did not glorify *Him* as God, nor were thankful, but became futile in their thoughts, and their foolish hearts were darkened. Professing to be wise, they became fools" (Romans 1:18-22, NKJV).

Once again, we are told that the evidence of God's creation is clearly seen, so that if we reject it, we are *without excuse* in God's sight. We should glorify God and be thankful, but if we willingly reject Him, our understanding is affected, and we become as fools, believing foolish things.

Elihu clearly did believe in a Creator God, and speaks eloquently about God's power in various aspects of the natural world. He sums up in the last two verses of chapter 37: "As *for* the Almighty, we cannot find Him; *He is* excellent in power, *In* judgment and abundant justice; He does not oppress. Therefore men fear Him; He shows no partiality to any *who are* wise of heart." Thus we are brought back to one of the first steps in seeking God: "The fear of the LORD *is* the beginning of wisdom" (Proverbs 9:10a, NKJV).

13. God answers Job

Job chapters 38 - 41

Elihu's speeches, which we considered in the previous chapter, form an introduction to the answer that God Himself now gives to Job. As we have seen in previous chapters, Job had wanted to speak directly with God, and to plead his cause. Now the moment has arrived! It is rather different to what Job had predicted. Right at the end of his speeches, Job had said "Oh, that I had one to hear me! Here is my mark. *Oh, that* the Almighty would answer me, *That* my Prosecutor had written a book! Surely I would carry it on my shoulder, *And* bind it on me *like* a crown; I would declare to Him the number of my steps; Like a prince I would approach Him" (Job 31:35-37, NKJV). Then, Job was convinced of his self-righteousness and his ability to stand before God in his own merits, but now the situation is rather different.

God starts abruptly, speaking out of the whirlwind, and He asks "Who *is* this who darkens counsel By words without knowledge?" (verse 2, NKJV). Job and his friends had spent a long time arguing, but really, in God's sight, Job's arguments had been "words without knowledge", and as a result, he had "darkened counsel" — he had confused and obscured the issues. The fact that God spoke out of a whirlwind is significant. A stormy wind is suggestive of judgement, and God was going to judge Job's words. We know that God's love for Job was always present and active, and that God's desire was to bless Job as a result of all these circumstances, but at this moment in time, Job needed to learn that what he had been saying was not right.

In considering God's answer to Job, I am very mindful of what C. H. Mackintosh wrote on this passage:

> "... God Himself begins to deal directly with the soul of His servant (chapters 38-41). He appeals to His works in creation as the display of a power and wisdom which ought assuredly to make Job feel his own littleness. We do not attempt to cull passages from one of the most magnificent and sublime sections of the inspired canon. It must be read as a whole. It needs no comment. The human finger could but tarnish its lustre. Its plainness is only equalled by its moral grandeur." [8].

Mindful of the advice quoted, I will just consider some important points. God, as has been said, appeals to His works, and clearly shows the interest that He has in His creation. Many aspects of the natural world are brought out, and it is clear that God is no passive onlooker but takes an active concern of all that He has made, including places where man has not set his foot (see Job 38:25-27, for example). Clearly the force of God's answer to Job is that God is in control of the universe that He has made, and that He can therefore be trusted to deal with Job as is right. Job, on the other hand, who could not begin to measure up against such a record, had no right to criticise

God's dealings and charge Him with lack of concern or unfairness.

There is no doubt a great deal of further teaching that we can gain from a careful study of God's answer to Job. I will consider just three points below:

THE EXTENT OF GOD'S KNOWLEDGE AND POWER

God answers Job's challenge that God was unfair and unconcerned, and He does so by showing him His creatorial power. Job no doubt was made to feel his littleness when God asked questions such as "Where were you when I laid the foundations of the earth? Tell *Me*, if you have understanding" (Job 38:4, NKJV), "Have you commanded the morning since your days *began, And* caused the dawn to know its place?" (Job 38:12, NKJV), "Have you entered the springs of the sea? Or have you walked in search of the depths?" (Job 38:16, NKJV), and "Have you entered the treasury of snow, Or have you seen the treasury of hail?" (Job 38:22, NKJV).

Job 38:17 is particularly interesting, because here God goes beyond His control of the natural world, and asks Job "Have the gates of death been revealed to you? Or have you seen the doors of the shadow of death?" The knowledge of death and what comes afterwards has ever been that dark, unsolved and unwelcome mystery for men and women throughout the ages. But God knows all about it, and we can know all about it too, if we believe God's record to us in the Bible. I have spoken on this theme at several points throughout this commentary, because I believe that the great issues of death, judgement, redemption and resurrection are clearly prefigured in the book of Job. With the revelation of the New Testament, we can understand the hints and figures given in the book of Job, for our profit and blessing. One of the reasons for writing this commentary was that any who read it may themselves be totally clear and assured about the issues of death and afterwards, in the knowledge that they are safe through the work of the Lord Jesus Christ. Jesus went into death for us — the gates of death were opened unto Him, to use the words of Job 38:17 — but He came out victorious, so that we can say the gates were opened to Him again, as He came out of death. We too can follow Him, if we trust in Him, and thus be clear of death and its penalty of judgement.

THE CHARACTER OF GOD

In Job chapter 40, God again challenges Job as to his earlier comments:

> "Then the LORD answered Job out of the whirlwind, and said: "Now prepare yourself like a man; I will question you, and you shall answer Me: "Would you indeed annul My judgment? Would you condemn Me that you may be justified? Have you an arm like God? Or can you thunder with a voice like His? Then adorn yourself *with* majesty and splendor, and array yourself with glory and beauty. Disperse the rage of your wrath; Look on everyone *who is* proud, and humble him. Look on everyone *who is* proud, *and* bring him low; Tread down the wicked in their place. Hide them in the dust together, Bind their faces in hidden *darkness*. Then I will also confess to you That your own right hand can save you."" (Job 40:6-14, NKJV).

God was taking issue with Job's argument that he was righteous, and that God was being unfair in the way that He was dealing with him. But God teaches Job about His dealings with men — He has glory and majesty, and He brings down the proud and the wicked. "Can you do the same?" asks God; "Do you also deal with the proud and wicked?" Thus God is not only the Creator of the universe, but the moral Governor also. In both cases therefore He has the ability and the right to act, and Job should not have questioned this.

BEHEMOTH AND LEVIATHAN

Job chapter 40:15 - 41:34 speaks of two mysterious creatures, *behemoth* and *leviathan*. Various ideas have been put forward as to what they might be. The description of the behemoth sounds rather like a dinosaur, but we have no further clues since this animal is only mentioned here in the Bible. Leviathan sounds more like a dragon, and it is mentioned elsewhere in the Bible: twice in the Psalms[a], and once in Isaiah (quoted below):

> "In that day the LORD with His severe sword, great and strong, Will punish Leviathan the fleeing serpent, Leviathan that twisted serpent; And He will slay the reptile that *is* in the sea." (Isaiah 27:1, NKJV).

I am sure that there is a spiritual and moral significance to this passage about leviathan (which takes up all of Job chapter 41), rather than simply being a description of what seems to be a sea-dragon. The passage in Isaiah quoted above speaks of God *punishing* leviathan. This suggests that leviathan, the *twisted serpent*, must be symbolical of *someone* who is to be punished. The figures of a serpent and a dragon are often used in the Bible to represent Satan. We have this clearly stated in Revelation, firstly in chapter 12 verse 9: "So the great dragon was cast out, that serpent of old, called the Devil and Satan, who deceives the whole world; he was cast to the earth, and his angels were cast out with him" and again in chapter 20 verse 2: "He laid hold of the dragon, that serpent of old, who is *the* Devil and Satan, and bound him for a thousand years". Thus I believe that in the description of leviathan here in Job chapter 41, we can learn something about Satan.

There are a great many things that could be brought out from the description of leviathan, but let us consider the following few points. The final verse tells us that "He beholds every high *thing*; **He *is* king over all the children of pride**" (verse 34, NKJV; emphasis mine). Pride is particularly connected with Satan. We are told in 1 Timothy 3:6 that pride is the condemnation of the devil. Ezekiel chapter 28 speaks about the King of Tyre, also a symbolic passage about the devil, and in verse 17 we read "Your heart was lifted up because of your beauty; You corrupted your wisdom for the sake of your splendor; I cast you to the ground, I laid you before kings, That they might gaze at you" — an indication that it was pride that led to the initial downfall of the devil. The devil now deceives us with pride — it is pride that leads us to think that we are good enough for God, or that our good deeds will suffice for Him, rather than accepting what God says, namely that we are sinners who deserve judgement, but that full and free forgiveness is available in the Lord Jesus Christ.

The devil may deceive us, but he also seeks to terrify. We are told that the Lord Jesus became a man so "Inasmuch then as the children have partaken of flesh and blood, He Himself likewise shared in the same, that through death He might destroy **him who had the power of death, that is, the devil**, and **release those who through fear of death were all their lifetime subject to bondage**" (Hebrews 2:14-15, NKJV; emphasis mine). These verses portray the devil as one who keeps men and women in bondage through fear of death. It also speaks of the Lord

Jesus Christ, who came to destroy the power of the devil and deliver us. I believe we can see some aspects of this battle in the description of leviathan that we have here in Job chapter 41. In verses 8-9 we read "Lay your hand on him; Remember the battle— Never do it again! Indeed, *any* hope of *overcoming* him is false; Shall *one not* be overwhelmed at the sight of him?" We have here the description of a formidable and terrifying enemy: *shall one not be overwhelmed at the sight of him?* Who indeed will dare to fight with this enemy of humankind, who desires and seeks to drag with himself as many as possible into eternal condemnation? By keeping men and women in ignorance of what the Lord Jesus has done, by keeping them in bondage to superstition, false religions, and a host of other things that men and women will seek to do *through fear of death*, in the hope that they will be all right, the devil keeps a tight grip. He is called "the god of this age" who has blinded the minds of those "who do not believe, lest the light of the gospel of the glory of Christ, who is the image of God, should shine on them" (2 Corinthians 4:4, NKJV). The devil does not want to lose his prey, and will do whatever is necessary to keep men and women from believing the glorious good news that Jesus Christ has accomplished a full and free redemption for all.

Who then will fight against this leviathan? The Lord Jesus has won the battle against our formidable enemy. The devil might well be the "strong man" who keeps a tight hold of his goods (see Luke 11:21, NKJV), but the Lord Jesus is the "stronger than he" who came upon him, overcame him and "takes from him all his armor in which he trusted, and divides his spoils" (see Luke 11:22, NKJV). We have another picture of the devil in the well-known story of David and Goliath (for details of this account see 1 Samuel chapter 17). Goliath, like leviathan, was a terrifying enemy whom no-one dared to attack. But David, who is a picture of the Lord Jesus, ran to meet him (see 1 Samuel 17:48) and defeated him. The Lord Jesus defeated Satan on the cross. The Lord Jesus had to lay down His life in that battle, but because He paid the penalty for *our* sins, and was raised again by the Father, *we* can be free. No longer do we need to be in "fear of death" — there is no fear for those who benefit from the Lord's victory. 1 Corinthians 15:56 tells us "The sting of death *is* sin, and the strength of sin *is* the law." The devil knows that we have sinned, and seeks to keep us in bondage — what will come after death? And thus many are caught up in seeking to do good works, following empty religions, or trying to drown their fears and conscience in business, pleasure, or anything else. And so the devil keeps his prey. But he has been defeated! The next verse in 1 Corinthians 15 tells us "But thanks *be* to God, who gives us the victory through our Lord Jesus Christ." The devil, who is the "accuser of the brethren" (see Revelation 12:10) may well seek to terrify us by bringing our sins to remembrance, but if we have believed on the Lord Jesus and accepted His forgiveness, then we have been justified and have nothing to fear. "Who shall bring a charge against God's elect? *It is* God who justifies. Who *is* he who condemns? *It is* Christ who died, and furthermore is also risen, who is even at the right hand of God, who also makes intercession for us" (Romans 8:33-34, NKJV).

I believe that it is significant that God ends His speech to Job by speaking of the terrible dragon leviathan and the battle against him. Surely the work of the Lord Jesus on the cross, by which He defeated the devil and the power of death, so that we sinners might be forgiven, justified and glorified with Him, surely this is the most marvellous and praiseworthy of all the works of God.

14. Conclusion: Job's restoration

We have now reached the end of our study of Job. After having read many lengthy speeches and answers, Job's final confession is strikingly brief — just six verses. However, there is a great deal in these six verses. In many ways they are more valuable than the very large number of verses that Job had used in justifying himself. Job starts by confessing God's sovereignty and power: "Then Job answered the LORD and said: "I know that You can do everything, And that no purpose *of Yours* can be withheld from You" (verses 1-2, NKJV). If God is minded to do something, there is nothing that can prevent it. Proverbs 21:30 clearly states that "*There is* no wisdom or understanding Or counsel against the LORD." If it is true that God cannot be hindered in any of His thoughts, how wonderful is the fact that His thoughts towards us are ones of love! It is true that those who refuse to submit to God's declaration that they are sinners and need a Saviour cannot benefit from God's thoughts of love: "the wrath of God abides on him" (John 3:36b, NKJV). But God does not desire it to be that way: God is "**not willing** that any should perish but that all should come to repentance"

(2 Peter 3:9b, KJV; emphasis mine) and He "desires all men to be saved and to come to the knowledge of the truth" (1 Timothy 2:4, NKJV). If we are saved, then we can count on God's thoughts of love towards us: "How precious also are Your thoughts to me, O God! How great is the sum of them! *If* I should count them, they would be more in number than the sand; When I awake, I am still with You" (Psalm 139:17-18, NKJV).

Having acknowledged God's supreme power and sovereignty, Job realises that he had not been speaking rightly of God beforehand. God had answered Job, as we saw in Job chapters 38-41, and Job had understood that God both had the *right* to do as He pleased, and that what God did do *was* right. Job therefore uses God's own words against himself now: "*You asked*, 'Who *is* this who hides counsel without knowledge?' Therefore I have uttered what I did not understand, Things too wonderful for me, which I did not know" (verse 3; compare Job 38:2, NKJV). Job now saw things in God's light. Like Isaiah who, when in the presence of God, said "Woe *is* me, for I am undone! Because I *am* a man of unclean lips, And I dwell in the midst of a people of unclean lips; For my eyes have seen the King, The LORD of hosts" (Isaiah 6:5, NKJV), Job similarly says "Therefore I abhor *myself*, And repent in dust and ashes" (verse 6, NKJV).

To be able to truly say "therefore I *abhor* myself" is not easy. It meant that Job really did find himself abhorrent. We may be able to admit this in a theoretical way, because we know that the Bible says that "**all** have sinned" (see Romans 3:23, NKJV), that there "is **none** who does good, **no, not one**" (see Romans 3:12, NKJV; emphasis mine), and that "The heart *is* deceitful above all *things*, And desperately wicked; Who can know it?" (see Jeremiah 17:9, NKJV). These statements relate to what the Bible calls the *flesh*, i.e. what we really are as natural men before we are born again. We know that the flesh is abhorrent to God, because Romans 8:8 tells us that "those who are in the flesh **cannot please God**" (emphasis mine). Furthermore, we can understand from Romans 8:3 that the Lord Jesus Christ died on the cross so that God could condemn sin in the flesh: "…sending His own Son in the likeness of sinful flesh, on account of sin: He condemned sin in the flesh". The Lord Jesus took our sins *and* our sinful nature on Himself when He went to the cross. There He took the punishment for our *sins*, and furthermore the root cause of them, *sin in the flesh*, was condemned there also.

We may know all these things just outlined in the paragraph above, but it is often a difficult lesson to truly apply it to ourselves. It is easy to admit on the one hand that the flesh, our sinful nature, is irremediably bad, while at the same time keep hoping that we ourselves are not *that* bad, really! The Apostle Paul had learnt this lesson. He said "For I know that in me (that is, in my flesh) nothing good dwells" (Romans 7:18a, NKJV). Knowing that God has condemned sin in the flesh at the cross, the Apostle Paul goes on to say "I have been crucified with Christ; it is no longer I who live, but Christ lives in me; and the *life* which I now live in the flesh I live by faith in the Son of God, who loved me and gave Himself for me" (Galatians 2:20, NKJV; see note[a]). Have I really learnt this lesson, to realise that in myself, without the power of God, there is no good thing, and that it cannot be pleasing to God?

Note that the Apostle Paul did not just say "I have been crucified with Christ". The question does not end with the judgement of our flesh. There is a positive side too — "the life which I now live in the flesh I live by faith in the

Son of God, who loved me and gave Himself for me". Yes, Paul agreed that his flesh was only evil before God, and that God had condemned it in the Person of the Lord Jesus Christ at the cross, and that therefore he could not hope to be pleasing to God if he just carried on in the flesh. But the point was that when Paul realised that his flesh had been judged and done away with in God's sight, he had a new life, a life which could be pleasing to God, a life which was on the principle of faith in a Person, who was none other than the Son of God who loved him so much that He had been willing to die for him[b].

This is indeed the great point. God wants us to agree with His estimation of our flesh, and agree with Him that it is worthless and only fit for judgement, so that He can grant us a new life, in His power, and in the strength of His love. In the same way, we see this symbolically with Job. The very moment that Job had uttered those words "Therefore I abhor myself, and repent in dust and ashes", God states that he has spoken rightly (verse 7), that He will accept Job (verse 8), and God gave Job twice as much as he had before (verse 10) and "blessed the latter days of Job more than his beginning" (verse 12).

What about Job's friends? We can see from verse 7 that God was not pleased with what they had been saying. They had not presented God in a true light. They had tried to accuse Job of having committed some dreadful crime, and saw God only as a punisher of evil and a rewarder of good — but their idea of "good" seems to be good "done in the flesh". As we have seen, God dealt with Job, not so that Job could be confronted with some terrible crime of his past, but rather to be confronted with himself — to realise, as the apostle Paul realised, that "in me (that is, in my flesh) nothing good dwells". Nevertheless, God is gracious, and He desired that these friends of Job would themselves be instructed in this way. Job prayed for his friends, as God had instructed, and all ended well. Still, it must have been humbling for Eliphaz, Bildad and Zophar, who had been trying so hard to convince Job that he had greatly sinned, to now have to seek Job's intercession for them before God!

In conclusion, we can consider these two verses: "And the LORD restored Job's losses when he prayed for his friends. **Indeed the LORD gave Job twice as much as he had before**" (verse 10, NKJV; emphasis mine) and "Now the LORD blessed the latter *days* of Job more than his beginning" (verse 12a, NKJV). Job had gone through terrible circumstances, but it had been for his profit and blessing, and he had gained much from it. We therefore have the same thought in the New Testament: "Indeed we count them blessed who endure. **You have heard of the perseverance of Job and seen the end** *intended by* **the Lord—that the Lord is very compassionate and merciful**" (James 5:11, NKJV; emphasis mine). The challenge for myself and my readers is that we may be able to learn the same lessons as Job, so that we may be able to say with Job "But He knows the way that I take; *When* He has tested me, I shall come forth as gold" (Job 23:10, NKJV) — not because we are anything in ourselves, but because we have learnt that all we need, and the only one we can boast in, is the Lord Jesus Himself.

References

[1] *Concise Bible Dictionary.* Bible Truth Publishers, 59 Industrial Road, P.O. Box 649, Addison, Illinois 60101, USA.

[2] R. E. Baughman, *Seeking Bible Treasures.* Emmaus Bible School, Carlett Boulevard, Eastham, Wirral, Merseyside, UK. (1965).

[3] F. C. Jennings, *Satan: his Person, Work, Place and Destiny.* Loizeaux Brothers, Neptune, New Jersey, USA. (1975). ISBN 0-87213-422-9.

[4] Sir Robert Anderson, *The Silence of God.* Kregel Publications, Grand Rapids, Michigan, USA. (1978). ISBN 0-8254-2128-4.

[5] Rebecca Conolly and Russell Grigg. Flood! *Creation ex nihilo* vol. 23 no. 1 (Dec. 2000 - Feb. 2001 issue), pp. 26-30. ISSN 0819-1530.

[6] Useful information can be found at Answers in Genesis (www.answersingenesis.org) and Creation Ministries International (www.creationontheweb.com).

[7] W. J. ReMine, *The Biotic Message: Evolution versus Message Theory.* St. Paul Science, Saint Paul, Minnesota MN 55128, USA (1993). ISBN 0-9637999-0-8.

[8] C. H. Mackintosh, *Job and his Friends.* Bible Truth Publishers, 59 Industrial Road, P.O. Box 649, Addison, Illinois 60101, USA.

[9] Roy and Revel Hession, *We would see Jesus.* CLC Publications, 51 The Dean, Alresford, Hants., UK (2005). ISBN 0-87508-586-5.

Notes

CHAPTER 1: INTRODUCTION

[a] "All Scripture *is* given by inspiration of God, and *is* profitable for doctrine, for reproof, for correction, for instruction in righteousness." (2 Timothy 3:16, NKJV)

[b] Furthermore, God Himself expresses His displeasure at their sayings at the end of the book: "And so it was, after the LORD had spoken these words to Job, that the LORD said to Eliphaz the Temanite, "My wrath is aroused against you and your two friends, for you have not spoken of Me *what is* right, as My servant Job *has*."" (Job 42:7, NKJV).

CHAPTER 2: THE UNSEEN CONFLICT

[a] "This is the genealogy of Noah. Noah was a just man, perfect in his generations." (Genesis 6:9, NKJV)

[b] "And Abram was ninety-nine years old, when Jehovah appeared to Abram, and said to him, I *am* the Almighty God: walk before my face, and be perfect." (Genesis 17:1, J. N. Darby translation)

[c] "For *it is* not possible that the blood of bulls and goats could take away sins. ... By that will we have been sancti-

fied through the offering of the body of Jesus Christ once *for all*." (Hebrews 10:4&10, NKJV)

[d] "'The devil, who deceived them, was cast into the lake of fire and brimstone where the beast and the false prophet *are*. And they will be tormented day and night forever and ever." (Revelation 20:10, NKJV)

[e] "Then He will also say to those on the left hand, 'Depart from Me, you cursed, into the everlasting fire **prepared for the devil and his angels**:'" (Matthew 25:41, NKJV; emphasis mine)

[f] "For God so loved the world that He gave His only begotten Son, **that whoever believes in Him should not perish but have everlasting life**." (John 3:16, NKJV; emphasis mine)

"The Lord is not slack concerning *His* promise, as some count slackness, but is longsuffering toward us, **not willing that any should perish but that all should come to repentance**." (2 Peter 3:9, NKJV; emphasis mine)

[g] "For God did not send His Son into the world to condemn the world, but that the world through Him might be saved. He who believes in Him is not condemned; but he who does not believe is condemned already, because he has not believed in the name of the only begotten Son of God." (John 3:17-18, NKJV)

[h] "So the great dragon was cast out, that serpent of old, called the Devil and Satan, who deceives the whole world; he was cast to the earth, and his angels were cast out with him. Then I heard a loud voice saying in heaven, "Now salvation, and strength, and the kingdom of our God, and the power of His Christ have come, for **the accuser of our brethren, who accused them before our God day**

and night, has been cast down." (Revelation 12:9-10, NKJV; emphasis mine)

[i] "For I delivered to you first of all that which I also received: that Christ died for our sins according to the Scriptures, and that He was buried, and that He rose again the third day according to the Scriptures," (1 Corinthians 15:3-4, NKJV)

"...us who believe in Him who raised up Jesus our Lord from the dead, who was delivered up because of our offenses, and was raised because of our justification. Therefore, having been justified by faith, we have peace with God through our Lord Jesus Christ," (Romans 4:24 *end* -25 & 5:1, NKJV)

CHAPTER 3: JOB'S FIRST COMPLAINT

[a] See for example references to the grave in the Psalms, such as the two below:

"For in death *there is* no remembrance of You; In the grave who will give You thanks?" (Psalm 6:5, NKJV)

"Shall Your lovingkindness be declared in the grave? *Or* Your faithfulness in the place of destruction?" (Psalm 88:11, NKJV)

[b] "For I know *that* my Redeemer lives, And He shall stand at last on the earth; And after my skin is destroyed, this *I know*, That in my flesh I shall see God" (Job 19:25-26, NKJV)

"Jesus said to her, "Your brother will rise again." Martha said to Him, "I know that he will rise again in the resurrection at the last day."" (John 11:23-24, NKJV)

[c] "Cursed *be* the day in which I was born! Let the day not be blessed in which my mother bore me! Let the man *be* cursed Who brought news to my father, saying, "A

male child has been born to you!" Making him very glad. And let that man be like the cities Which the LORD over-threw, and did not relent; Let him hear the cry in the morning And the shouting at noon, Because he did not kill me from the womb, That my mother might have been my grave, And her womb always enlarged *with me*. Why did I come forth from the womb to see labor and sorrow, That my days should be consumed with shame?" (Jeremiah 20:14-18, NKJV)

[d] In the account of Luke 16:19-31, Abraham in paradise has to inform the rich man in hell that "between us and you there is a great gulf fixed, so that those who want to pass from here to you cannot, nor can those from there pass to us." (verse 26, NKJV)

[e] "And we know that **all things** work together for good to those who love God, to those who are the called according to *His* purpose." (Romans 8:28, NKJV; emphasis mine)

CHAPTER 4: ELIPHAZ'S FIRST SPEECH AND JOB'S REPLY

[a] This is a principle found elsewhere in the Bible also. For example:

"Do not be deceived, God is not mocked; for whatever a man sows, that he will also reap." (Galatians 6:7, NKJV)

[b] "For the wisdom of this world is foolishness with God. For it is written, "He catches the wise in their *own* crafti-ness"" (1 Corinthians 3:19, NKJV)

[c] "And you have forgotten the exhortation which speaks to you as to sons: "My son, do not despise the chastening of the LORD, Nor be discouraged when you are rebuked by Him; For whom the LORD loves He chastens, And scourges every son whom He receives."" (Hebrews 12:5-6, NKJV).

The above words are actually a quotation of Proverbs 3:11-12, but the thought is very similar to that expressed by Eliphaz.

[d] "For He has not put the world to come, of which we speak, in subjection to angels. But one testified in a certain place, saying: "What is man that You are mindful of him, Or the son of man that You take care of him? You have made him a little lower than the angels; You have crowned him with glory and honor, And set him over the works of Your hands. You have put all things in subjection under his feet." For in that He put all in subjection under him, He left nothing *that is* not put under him. But now we do not yet see all things put under him. But we see Jesus, who was made a little lower than the angels, for the suffering of death crowned with glory and honor, that He, by the grace of God, might taste death for everyone. For it was fitting for Him, for whom *are* all things and by whom *are* all things, in bringing many sons to glory, to make the captain of their salvation perfect through sufferings." (Hebrews 2:5-10, NKJV)

[e] "The Lord ... not willing that any should perish but that all should come to repentance." (2 Peter 3:9, NKJV)

[f] "Then I saw a great white throne and Him who sat on it, from whose face the earth and the heaven fled away. And there was found no place for them. And I saw the dead, small and great, standing before God, and books were opened. And another book was opened, which is *the Book* of Life. **And the dead were judged according to their works, by the things which were written in the books.** The sea gave up the dead who were in it, and Death and Hades delivered up the dead who were in them. **And they were judged, each one according to his works.**" (Revelation 20:11-13, NKJV; emphasis mine)

[g] "for all have sinned and fall short of the glory of God" (Romans 3:23, NKJV)

CHAPTER 5: BILDAD'S FIRST SPEECH AND JOB'S REPLY

[a] The death of a Christian is often referred to as sleeping in the Bible. For example:

"These things He said, and after that He said to them, "Our friend Lazarus sleeps, but I go that I may wake him up." Then His disciples said, "Lord, if he sleeps he will get well." However, Jesus spoke of his death, but they thought that He was speaking about taking rest in sleep. Then Jesus said to them plainly, "Lazarus is dead."" (John 11:11-14, NKJV)

[b] I am of course not suggesting that we should be in the habit of despising the wisdom of spiritual and godly men and women who have preceded us. The New Testament contains many exhortations to respect the elders, for example 1 Peter 5:5 "Likewise you younger people, submit yourselves to *your* elders. Yes, all of *you* be submissive to one another, and be clothed with humility, for "God resists the proud, But gives grace to the humble."" and Hebrews 13:7 "Remember those who rule over you, who have spoken the word of God to you, whose faith follow, considering the outcome of *their* conduct." But we need to be discerning regarding *whom* we listen to, and not simply appeal to tradition.

[c] "For it is written: "*As* I live, says the LORD, Every knee shall bow to Me, And every tongue shall confess to God."" (Romans 14:11, NKJV)

"that at the name of Jesus every knee should bow, of those in heaven, and of those on earth, and of those under the earth" (Philippians 2:10; NKJV)

[d] ". . . when the Lord Jesus is revealed from heaven with His mighty angels, in flaming fire taking vengeance on those who do not know God, and on those who do not obey the gospel of our Lord Jesus Christ. These shall be punished with everlasting destruction from the presence of the Lord and from the glory of His power, when He comes, in that Day, to be glorified in His saints and to be admired among all those who believe, because our testimony among you was believed." (2 Thessalonians 1:7-10, NKJV)

[e] It is interesting to note that belief in God and His creation are assumed in Paul's argument set forth in Romans; there is no justification of creation as a valid scientific theory, or further arguments to support it. In fact Paul goes as far as to say that because of the witness of creation, men and women are without excuse if they do not believe in God. God assumes that a proper and true examination of the natural world will provide ample evidence for its Creator.

[f] "In the beginning was the Word, and the Word was with God, **and the Word was God**... And the Word became flesh and dwelt among us, and we beheld His glory, the glory as of the only begotten of the Father, full of grace and truth." (John 1:1 and 1:14, NKJV; emphasis mine)

"Let this mind be in you which was also in Christ Jesus, who, being in the form of God, did not consider it robbery to be equal with God" (Philippians 2:5-6, NKJV)

Chapter 6: Zophar's First Speech and Job's Reply

[a] "for all have sinned and fall short of the glory of God, **being justified freely by His grace through the redemption that is in Christ Jesus**, whom God set forth

as a propitiation by His blood, through faith, to demonstrate His righteousness, because in His forbearance God had passed over the sins that were previously committed, to demonstrate at the present time His righteousness, **that He might be just and the justifier of the one who has faith in Jesus**." (Romans 3:23-26, NKJV; emphasis mine)

[b] "Sheol" is the place of departed spirits. It is sometimes translated as "grave" in the NKJV.

[c] "But of Him you are in Christ Jesus, who became for us wisdom from God—and righteousness and sanctification and redemption" (1 Corinthians 1:30, NKJV)

[d] "Do not be afraid; I am the First and the Last. I *am* He who lives, and was dead, and behold, I am alive forevermore. Amen. And I have the keys of Hades and of Death." (Revelation 1:17b-18, NKJV). "Hades" is the place of departed spirits, and, without further specification, need not refer to a place of torment - it could be the place of rest for those who have died "in Christ", with their sins forgiven. In the Old Testament the equivalent thought is given by the word "sheol" - see note [b].

[e] In response to the Pharisees, who did not believe in Him, the Lord Jesus said: "I am going away, and you will seek Me, and will die in your sin. Where I go you cannot come." So the Jews said, "Will He kill Himself, because He says, 'Where I go you cannot come'?" And He said to them, "You are from beneath; I am from above. You are of this world; I am not of this world. Therefore I said to you that you will die in your sins; **for if you do not believe that I am *He*, you will die in your sins**." (John 8:21-24, NKJV; emphasis mine)

CHAPTER 7: ELIPHAZ'S SECOND SPEECH AND JOB'S REPLY

[a] "All Scripture *is* given by inspiration of God, and *is* profitable for doctrine, for reproof, for correction, for instruction in righteousness" (2 Timothy 3:16, NKJV).

CHAPTER 8: BILDAD'S SECOND SPEECH AND JOB'S REPLY

[a] "Inasmuch then as the children have partaken of flesh and blood, He Himself [i.e. the Lord Jesus] likewise shared in the same, that through death He might destroy him who had the power of death, that is, the devil, and release those who through fear of death were all their lifetime subject to bondage" (Hebrews 2:14-15, NKJV).

[b] "For whom the LORD loves He chastens, And scourges every son whom He receives" (Hebrews 12:6, NKJV).

"As many as I love, I rebuke and chasten. Therefore be zealous and repent" (Revelation 3:19, NKJV).

[c] It may seem strange to some readers that I should write that we were "enemies of God". However, Colossians 1:21 tells us that prior to conversion, we are just that: "And you, who once were alienated and enemies in your mind by wicked works, yet now He has reconciled". Also, Romans 8:7 tells us that "the carnal mind *is* enmity against God; for it is not subject to the law of God, nor indeed can be."

[d] A few examples are given here: "scapegoat", from the goat which symbolically carried away the sins of the Israelites on the day of atonement (see Leviticus chapter 16); "the writing on the wall", after the incident when the Babylonian king Belshazzar saw God's finger write his condemnation on the wall (see Daniel chapter 5); "the fly in the ointment" (see Ecclesiastes 10:1).

[e] According to J.N. Darby, the expression "are not satisfied with my flesh" would mean "slander me".

CHAPTER 9: ZOPHAR'S SECOND SPEECH AND JOB'S REPLY

[a] Psalm 73 is worth reading on this subject. Asaph, the psalmist, considers the subject of the wicked, how they *appear* to prosper, and yet what their end is. The secret is to see *as God sees*: thus we have in verse 17 of this Psalm **"Until I went into the sanctuary of God**; *Then* I understood their end" (emphasis mine).

CHAPTER 10: ELIPHAZ'S THIRD SPEECH AND JOB'S REPLY

[a] In Luke 17:7-10, the Lord Jesus is speaking to His disciples about service. In verse 10 we read "So likewise you, when you have done all those things which you are commanded, say, 'We are unprofitable servants. We have done what was our duty to do.'" That is *our* side of the affair, so to speak: if we are tempted to think what wonderful service we have been giving to the Lord, we need to remind ourselves that we are only doing what we ought to be doing anyway, with probably a lot left undone! The Lord, on the other hand, loves to reward us and acknowledge what we have done, even though He has given us the ability to do it in the first place. In Revelation chapter 22, right at the end of the Bible, He says "And behold, I am coming quickly, and My reward *is* with Me, to give to every one according to his work" (Revelation 22:12, NKJV). He is looking forward to rewarding those who belong to Him.

[b] Eliphaz seems to be referring to Noah's flood here. The story of Noah's flood is generally considered fanciful in the world today, and is not believed literally. However, the Lord Jesus Himself spoke of it in Matthew 24:36-39. It is interesting to note that there are many 'flood stories' in

cultures all around the world, which bear striking resemblance to the account in Genesis. For an account of this, see reference [5].

CHAPTER 12: ELIHU AND HIS SPEECH

[a] This is not really true, of course, in that God *is* concerned with all our actions. When Saul (later the Apostle Paul) was struck down by the great light on the road to Damascus, the words of the Lord Jesus to him were "Saul, Saul, why are you persecuting **Me**?" (Acts 9:4, NKJV; emphasis mine). Saul had been persecuting the early Christians, and the Lord Jesus said that this was equivalent to persecuting Him. Similarly, in Matthew 25:31-46, when the Lord Jesus told the parable of the sheep and the goats, anything done or not done to His disciples was equivalent to it being done or not done to Him personally.

[b] I am not suggesting that the creation/evolution debate is a side-issue: it is important to carefully consider the scientific basis for belief in creation, especially where evolution, which is basically a world view, has been taught and promoted as if it were a clearly established fact. The assumption that evolution is a true explanation for why we are here will totally undermine a belief in the Bible. Christians need not be afraid of science; true science and the Bible do not contradict. However, it is important to realise *why* we should be interested in these things — the fact is that God will hold us responsible to Him, for His word tells us that the evidence of His creation is clearly seen.

CHAPTER 13: GOD ANSWERS JOB

[a] "For God *is* my King from of old, Working salvation in the midst of the earth. You divided the sea by Your

strength; You broke the heads of the sea serpents in the waters. You broke the heads of Leviathan in pieces, And gave him as food to the people inhabiting the wilderness" (Psalm 74:12-14, NKJV).

"O LORD, how manifold are Your works! In wisdom You have made them all. The earth is full of Your possessions— This great and wide sea, In which *are* innumerable teeming things, Living things both small and great. There the ships sail about; *There is* that Leviathan Which You have made to play there" (Psalm 104:24-26, NKJV).

CHAPTER 14: CONCLUSION: JOB'S RESTORATION

[a] We need to be careful to distinguish what is meant by 'flesh' in the Bible. Sometimes it can mean what we are in ourselves, i.e. our sinful nature, but it can also refer to our human bodies generally, such as in the phrase "flesh and blood". The context will make it plain what is meant. In Galatians 2:20, "the life which I now live in the flesh" refers to Paul's human life, not the evil flesh that I have been describing in this chapter.

[b] Another area in which we need to be careful is the fact that a believer in God has *two* natures. He has a new nature, which Paul expressed as "Christ lives in me", which happens when he is born again. But the flesh, the old, sinful nature, *is still there.* If we agree with God's estimation that it is incurably evil, and we accept that in His sight, it has been condemned at the cross, we will not seek to do anything in the power of the flesh. This would mean *not expecting anything good to come of ourselves,* in that we know what the flesh is like, but rather relying on God's help to be able to live in the power of His life.

www.ingramcontent.com/pod-product-compliance
Lightning Source LLC
Chambersburg PA
CBHW030110070426
42448CB00036B/592